SEA CREATURES

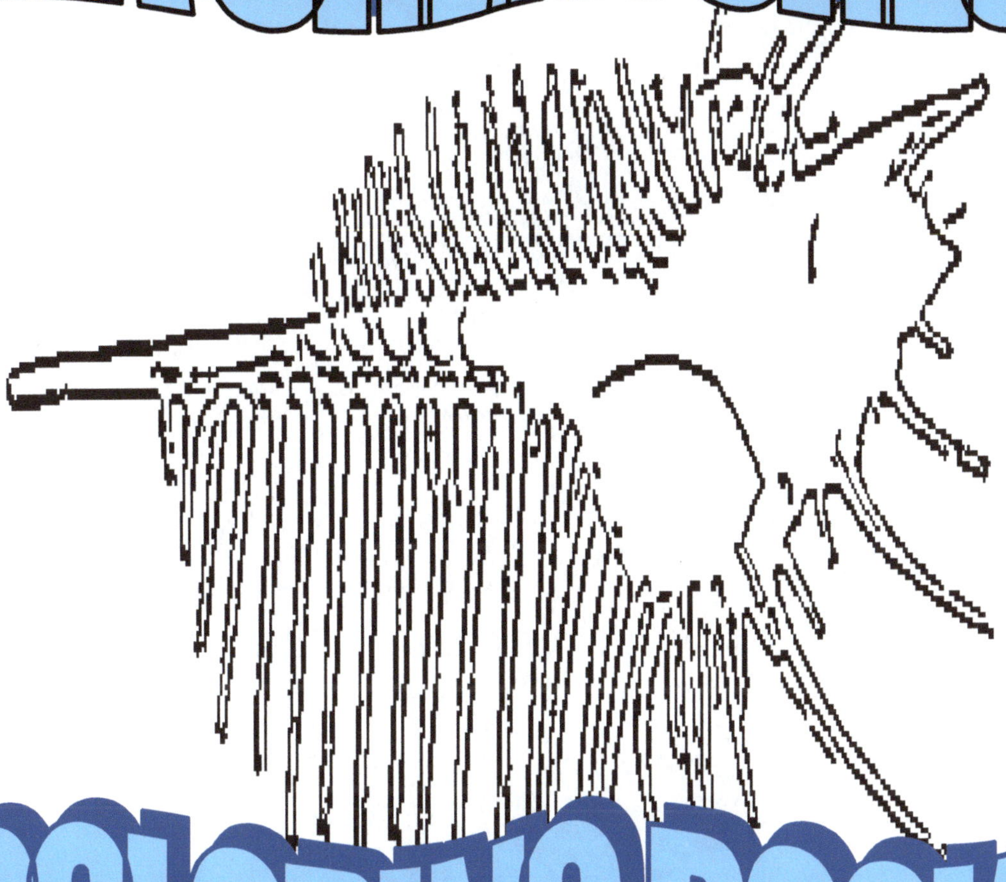

COLORING BOOK

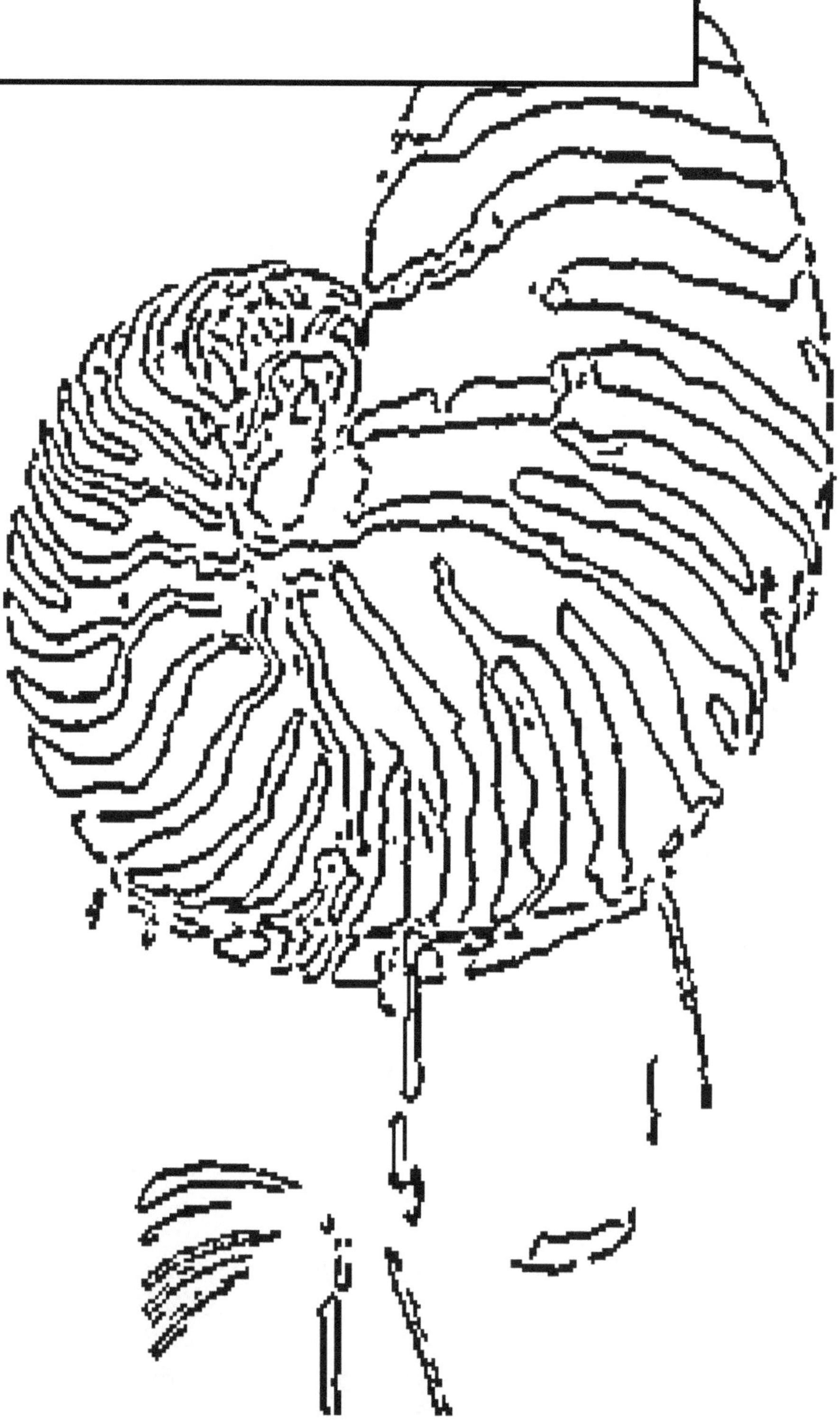

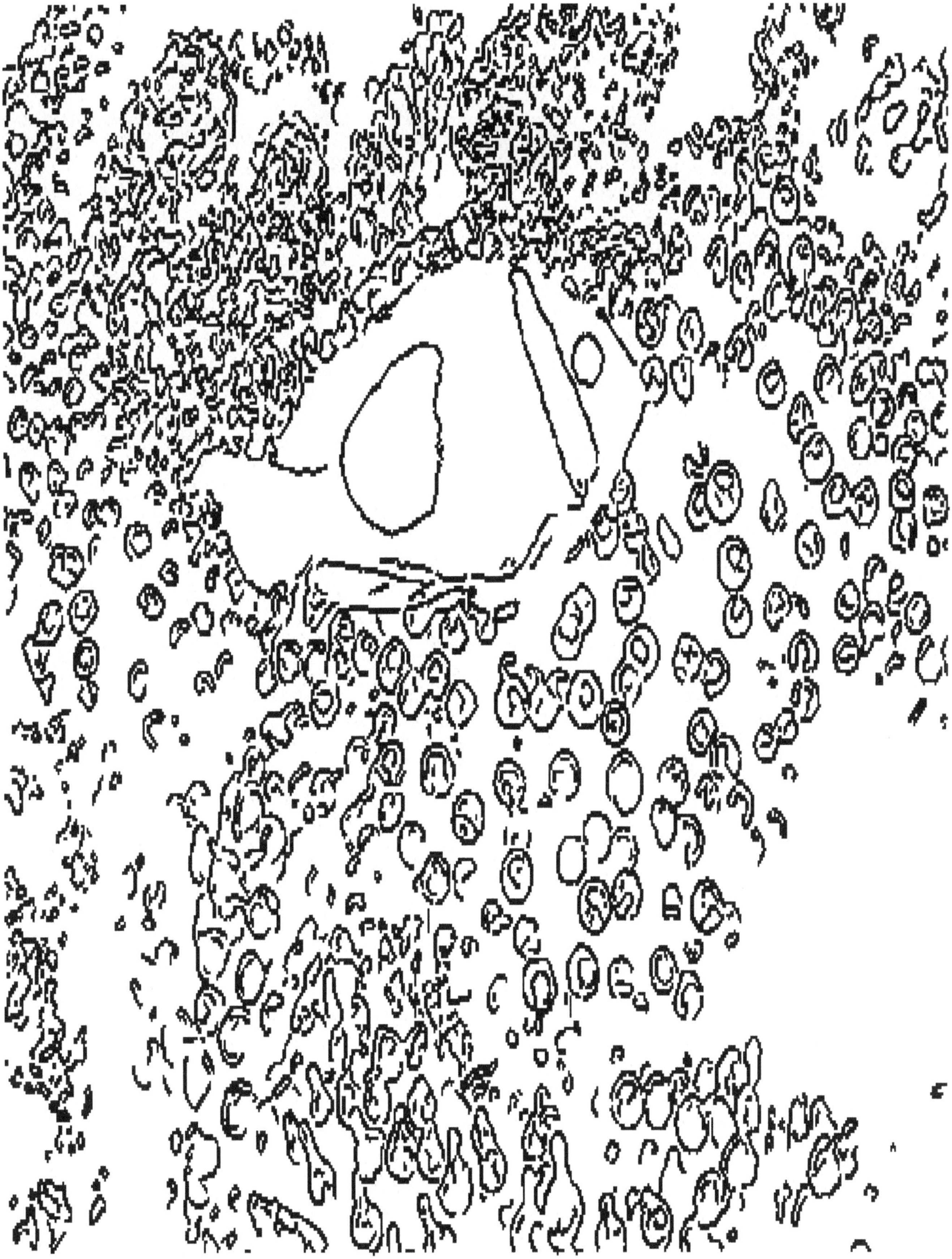

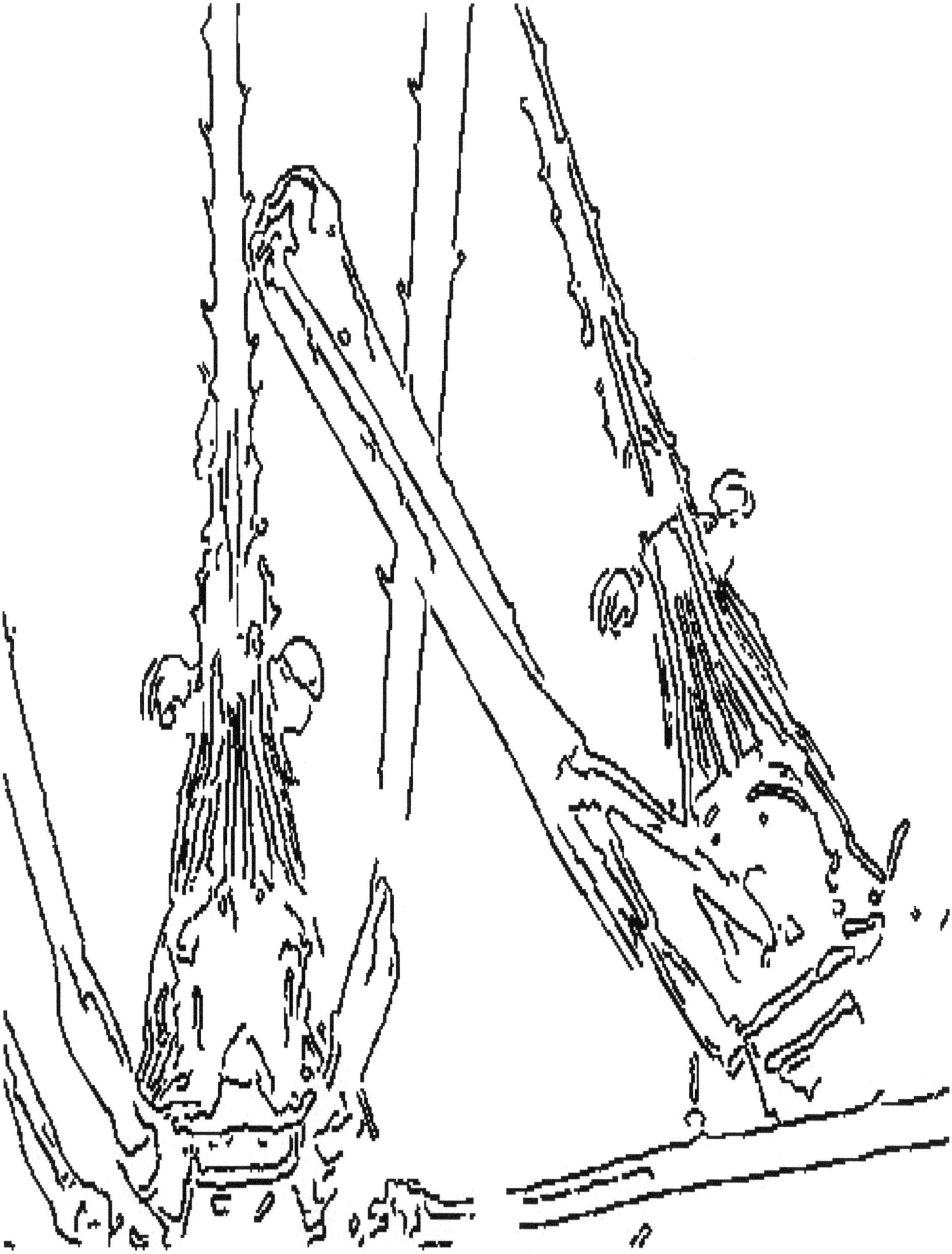

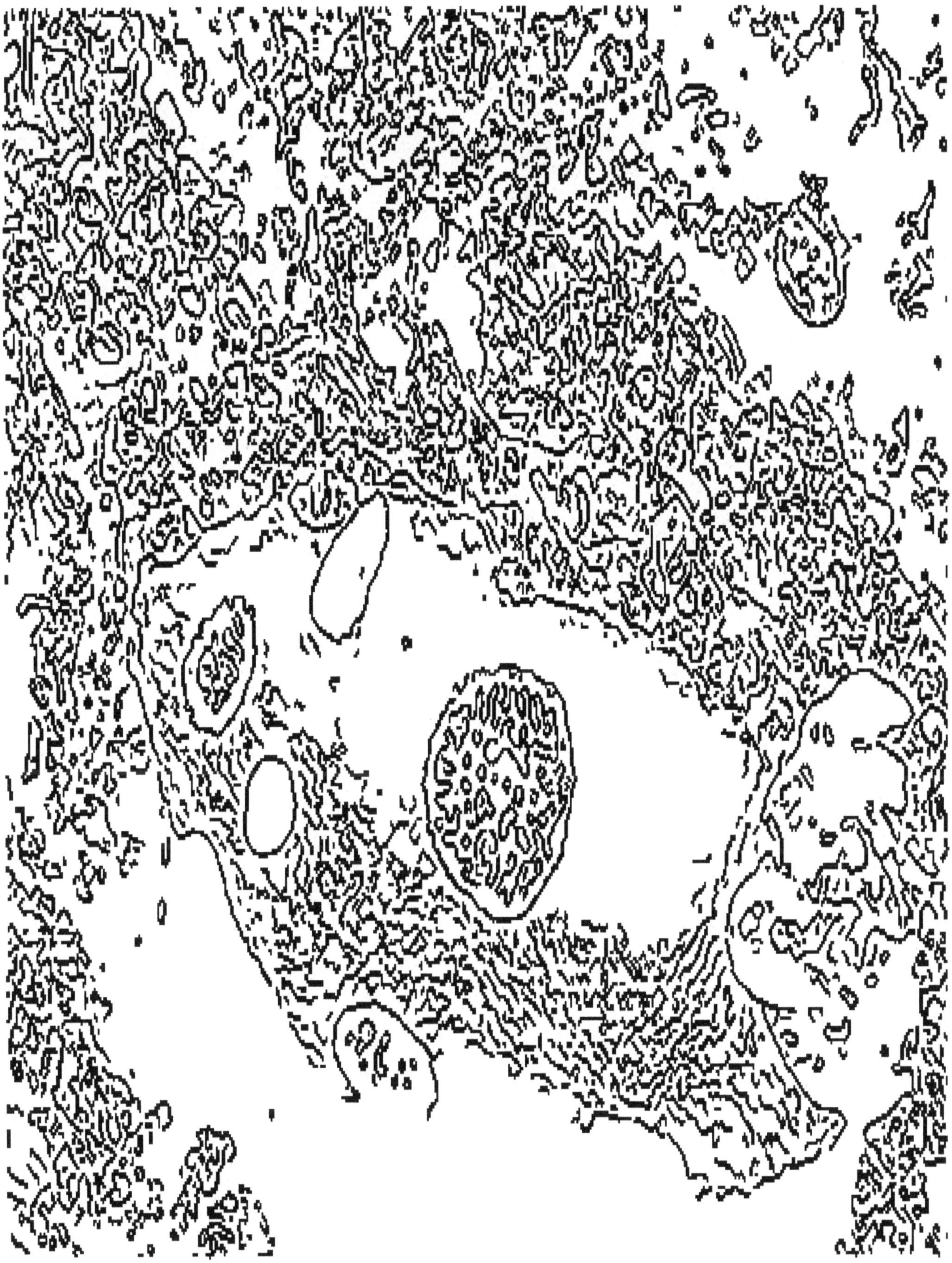

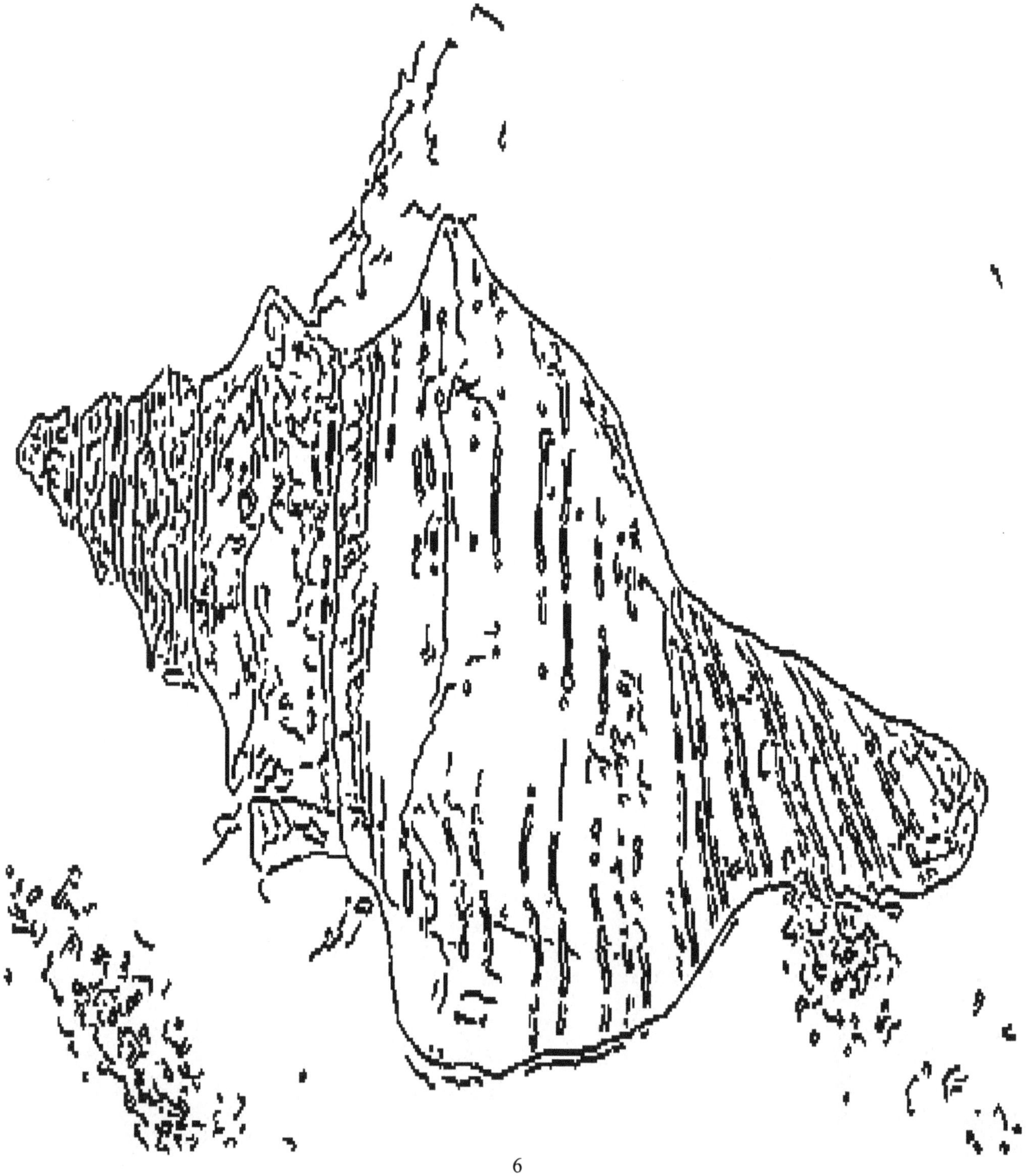

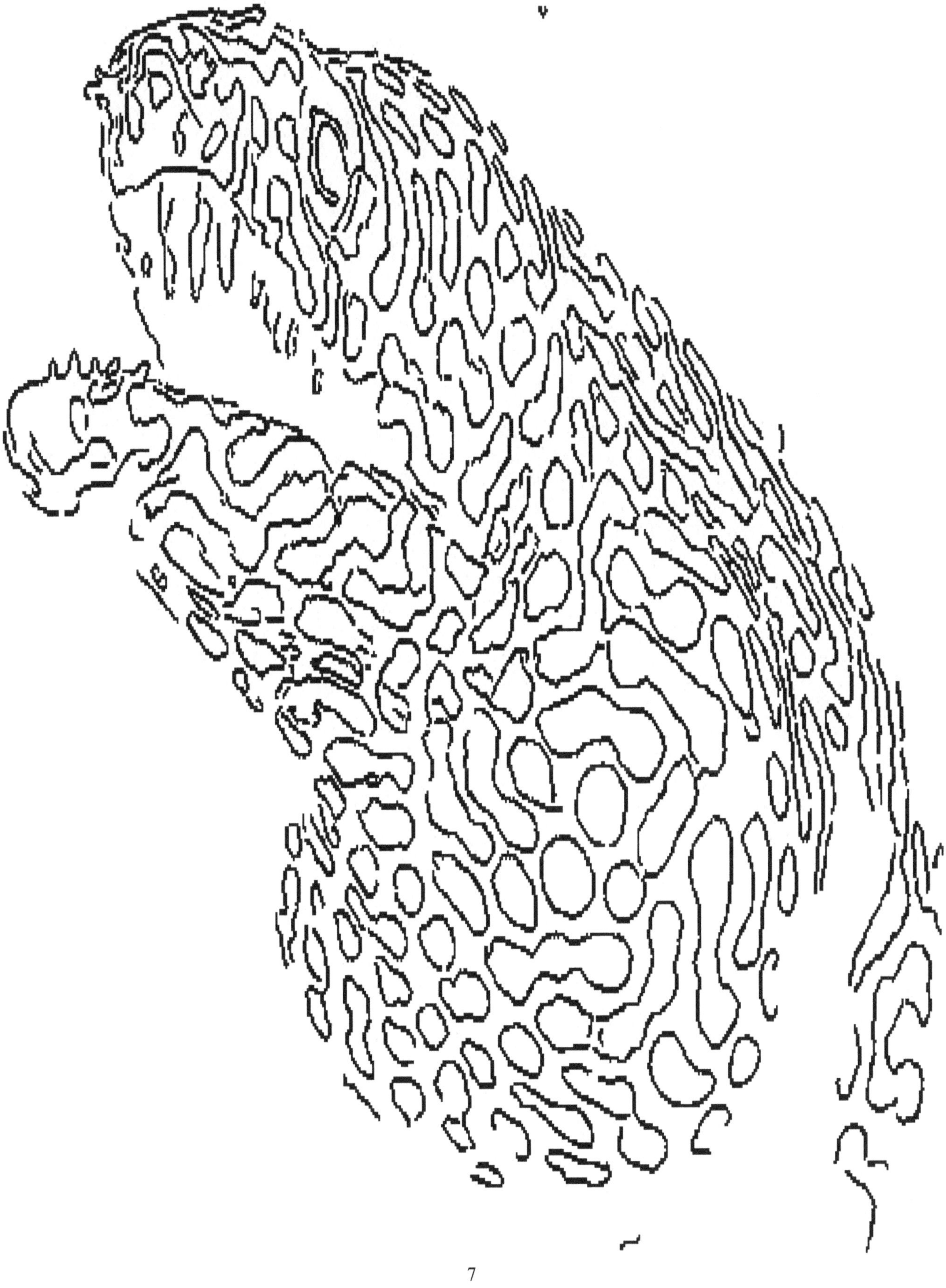

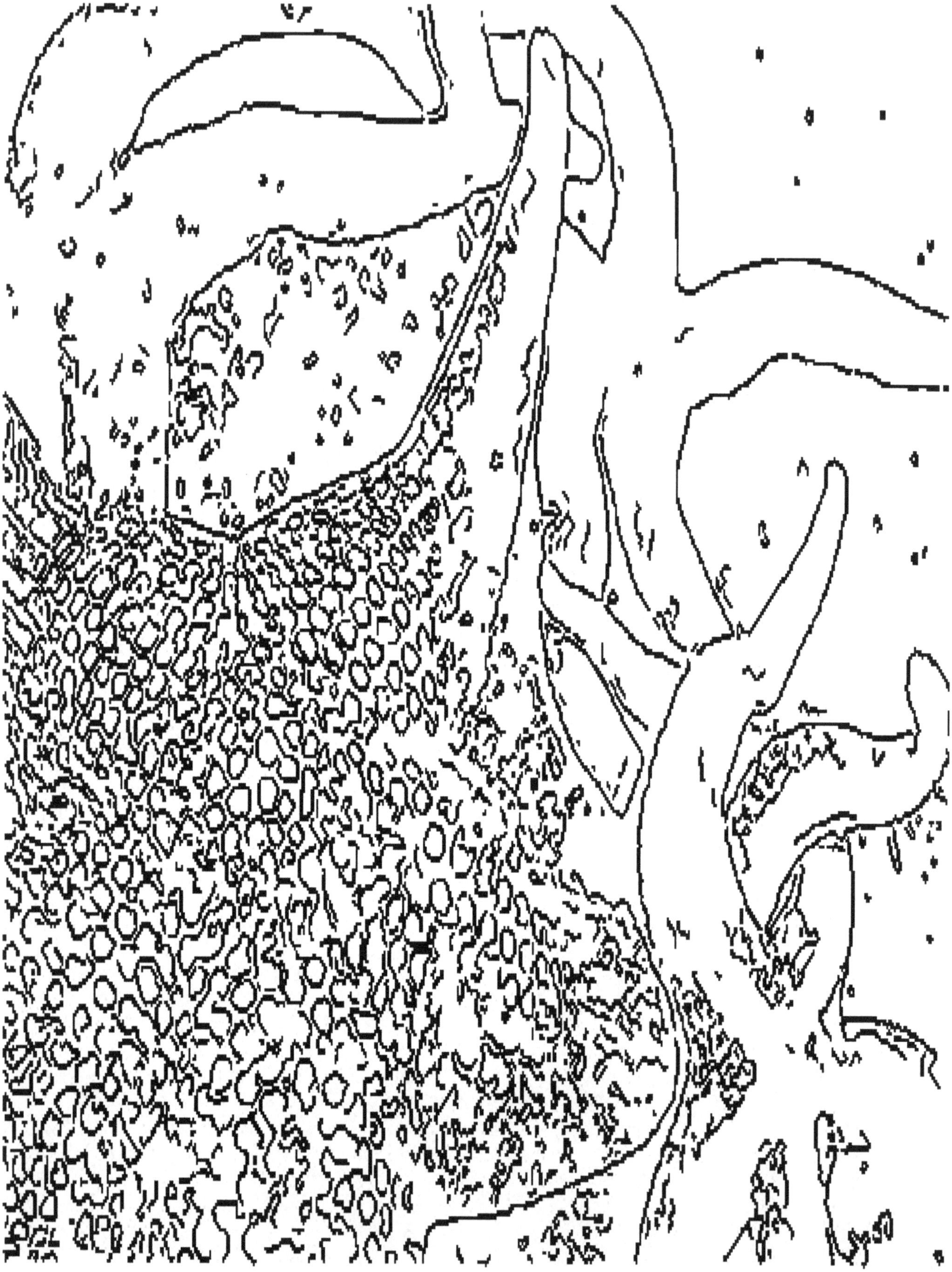

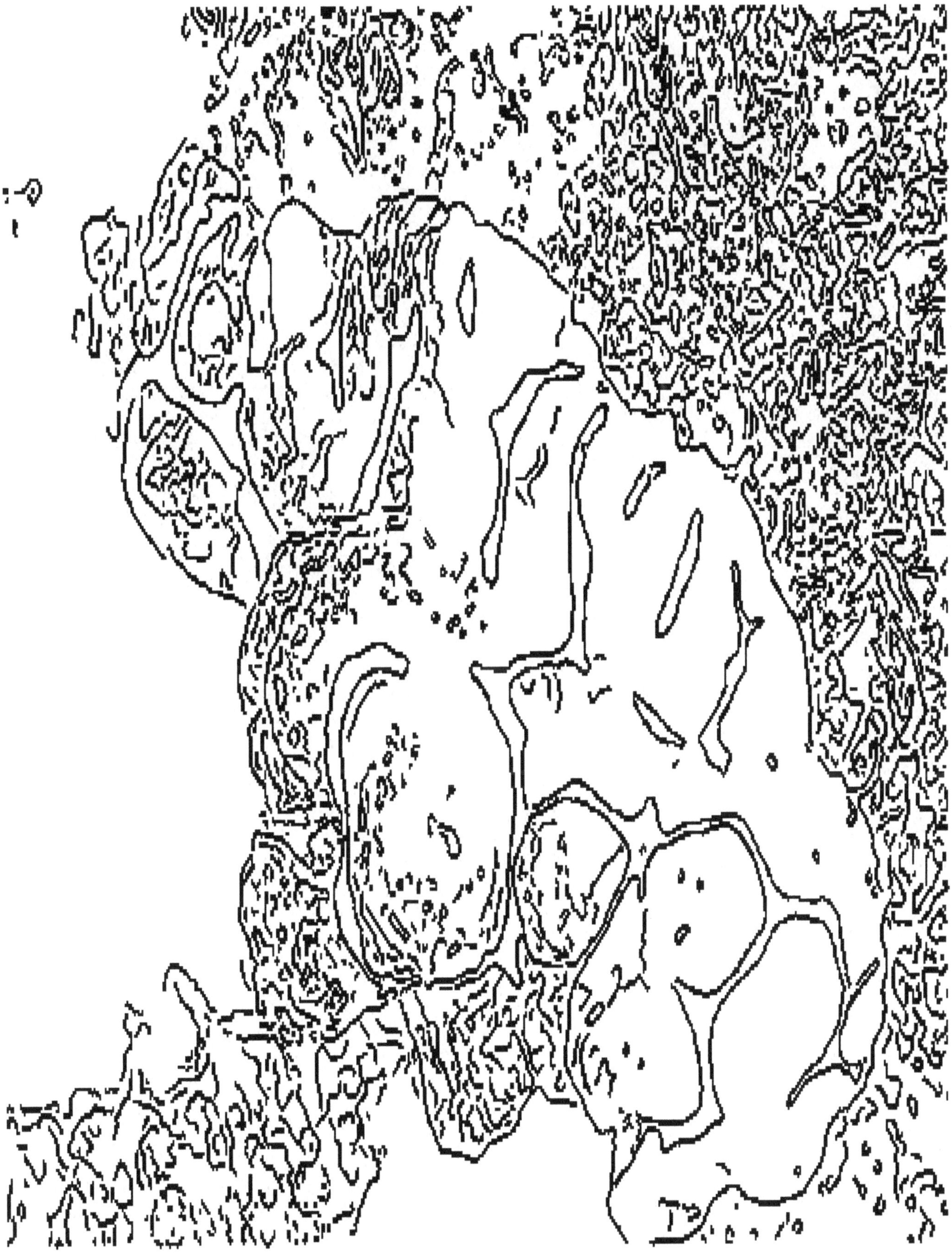

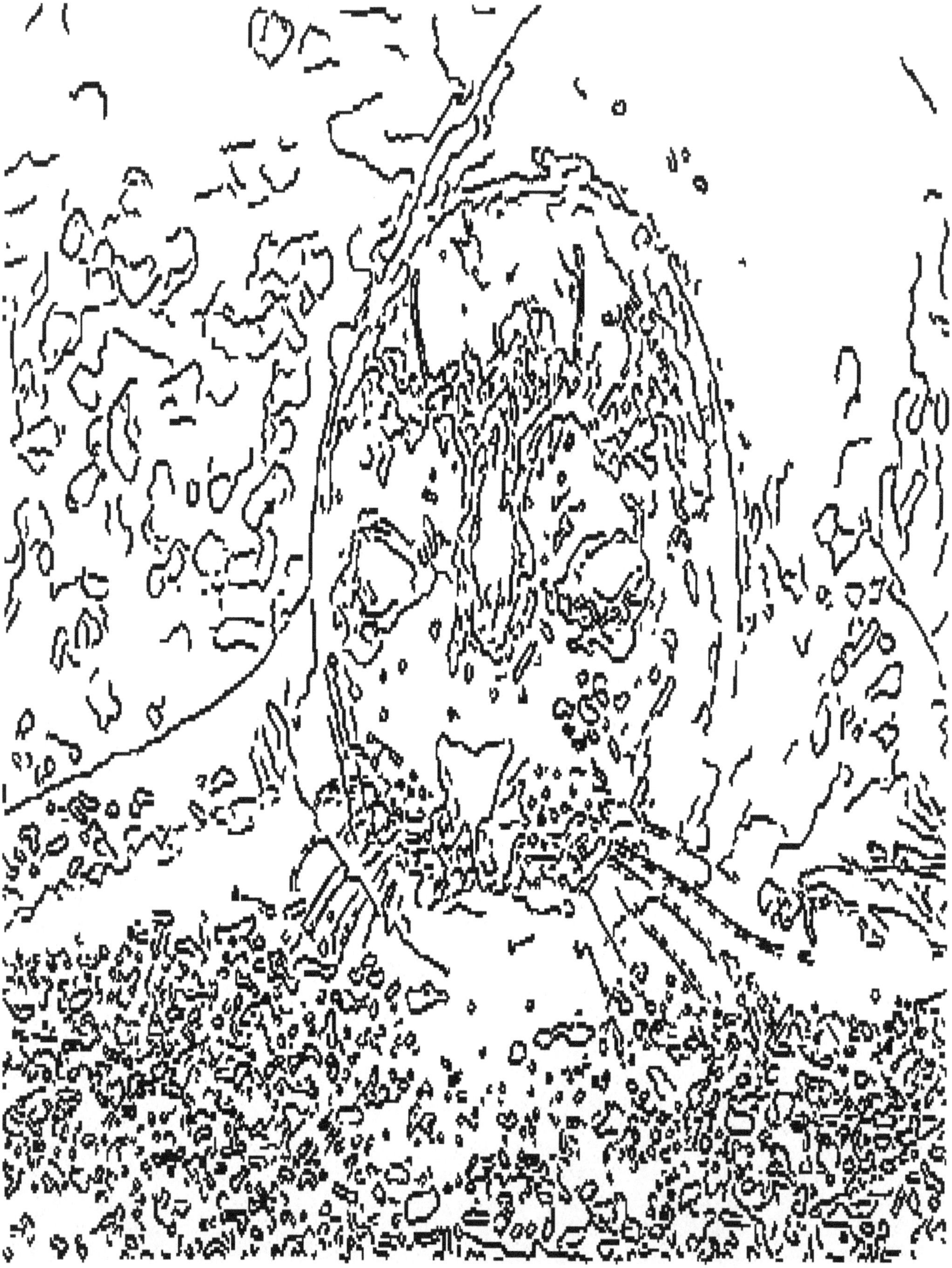

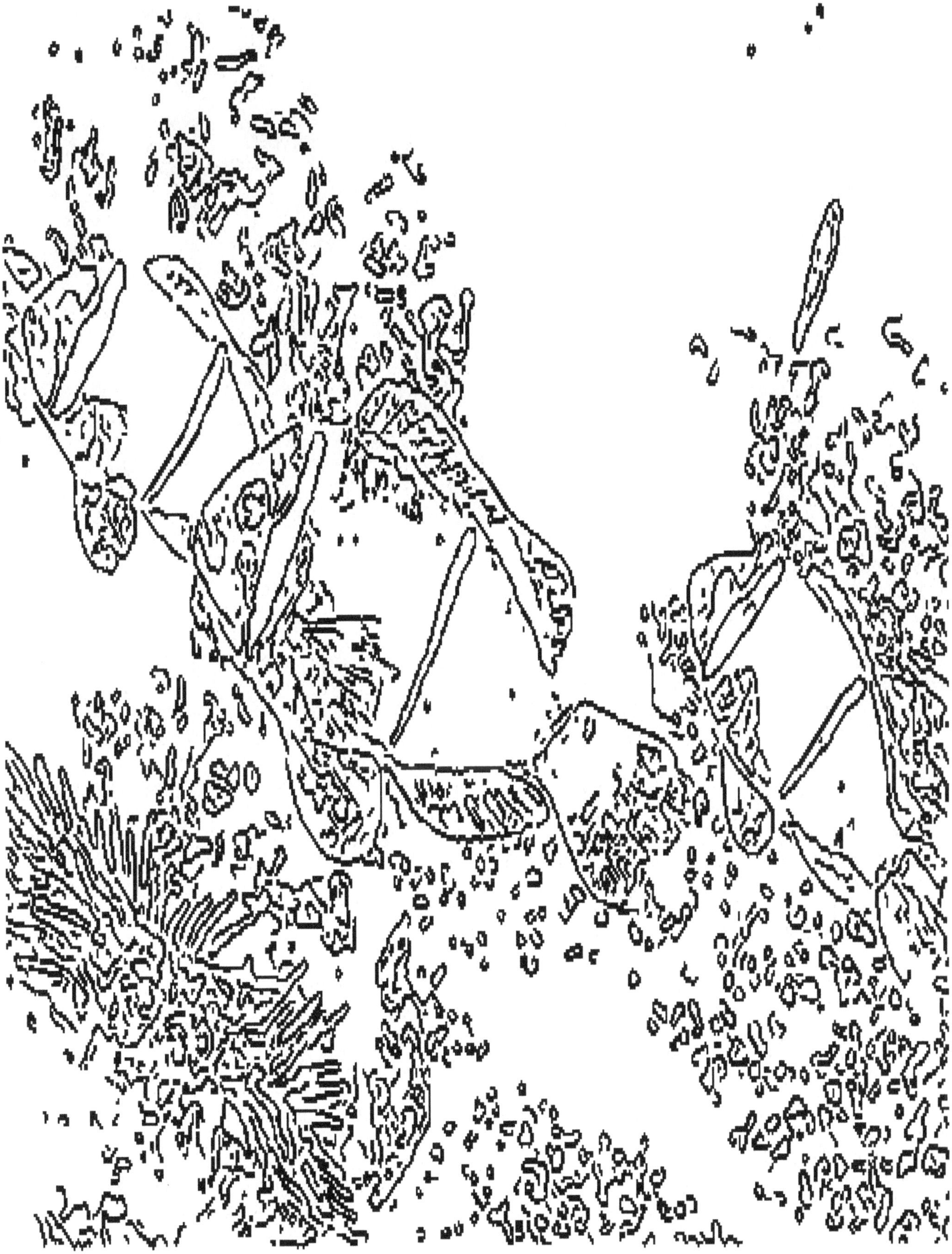

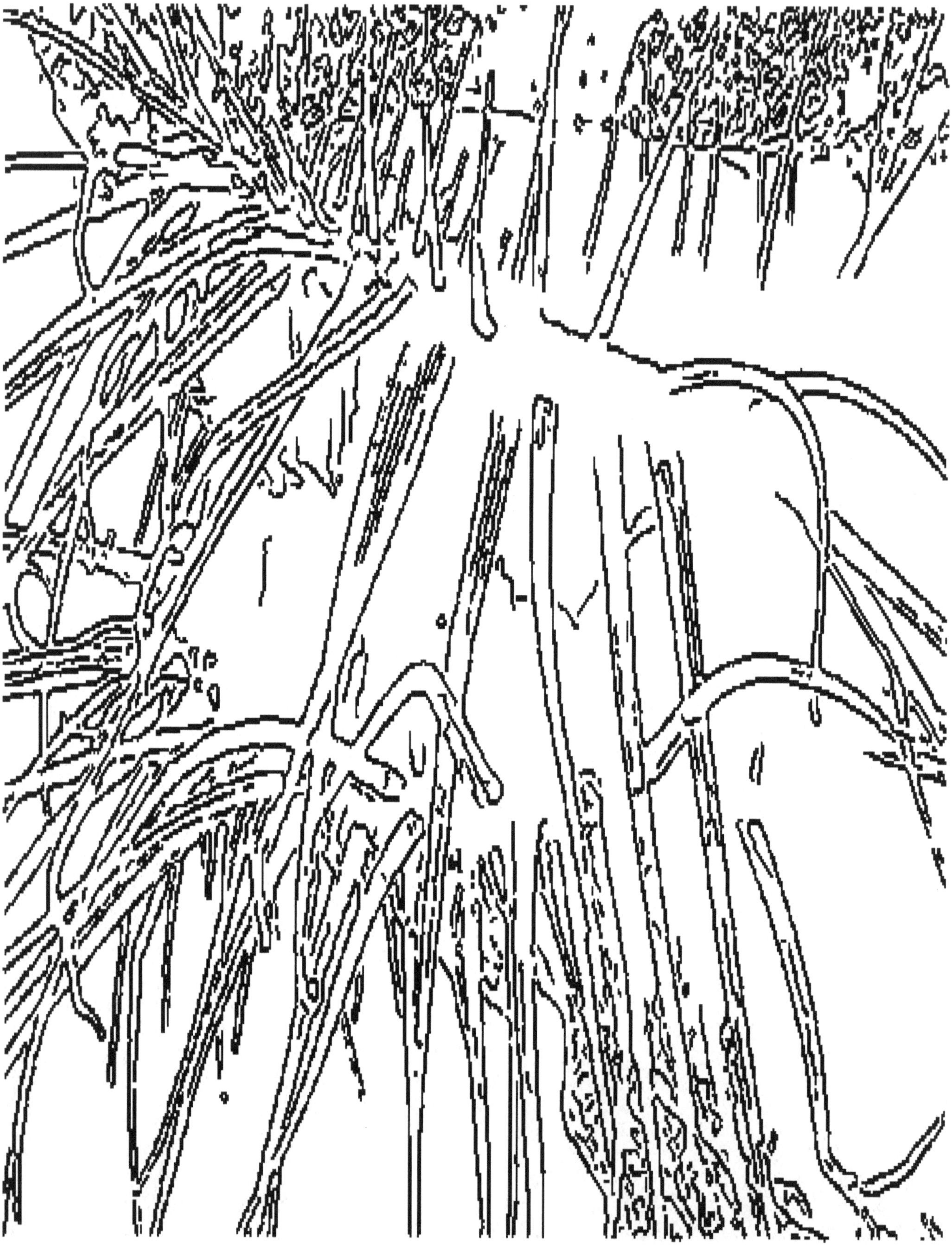

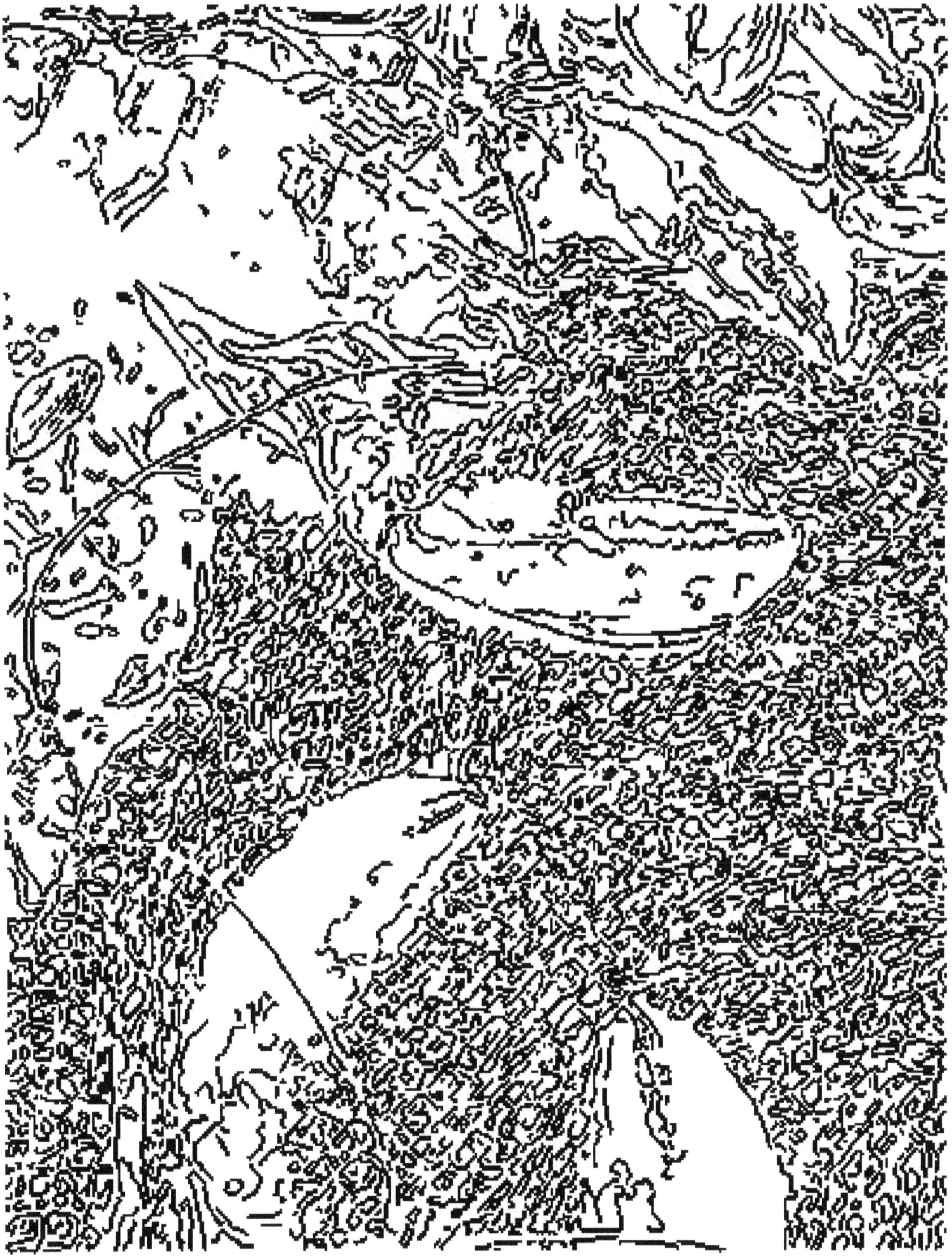

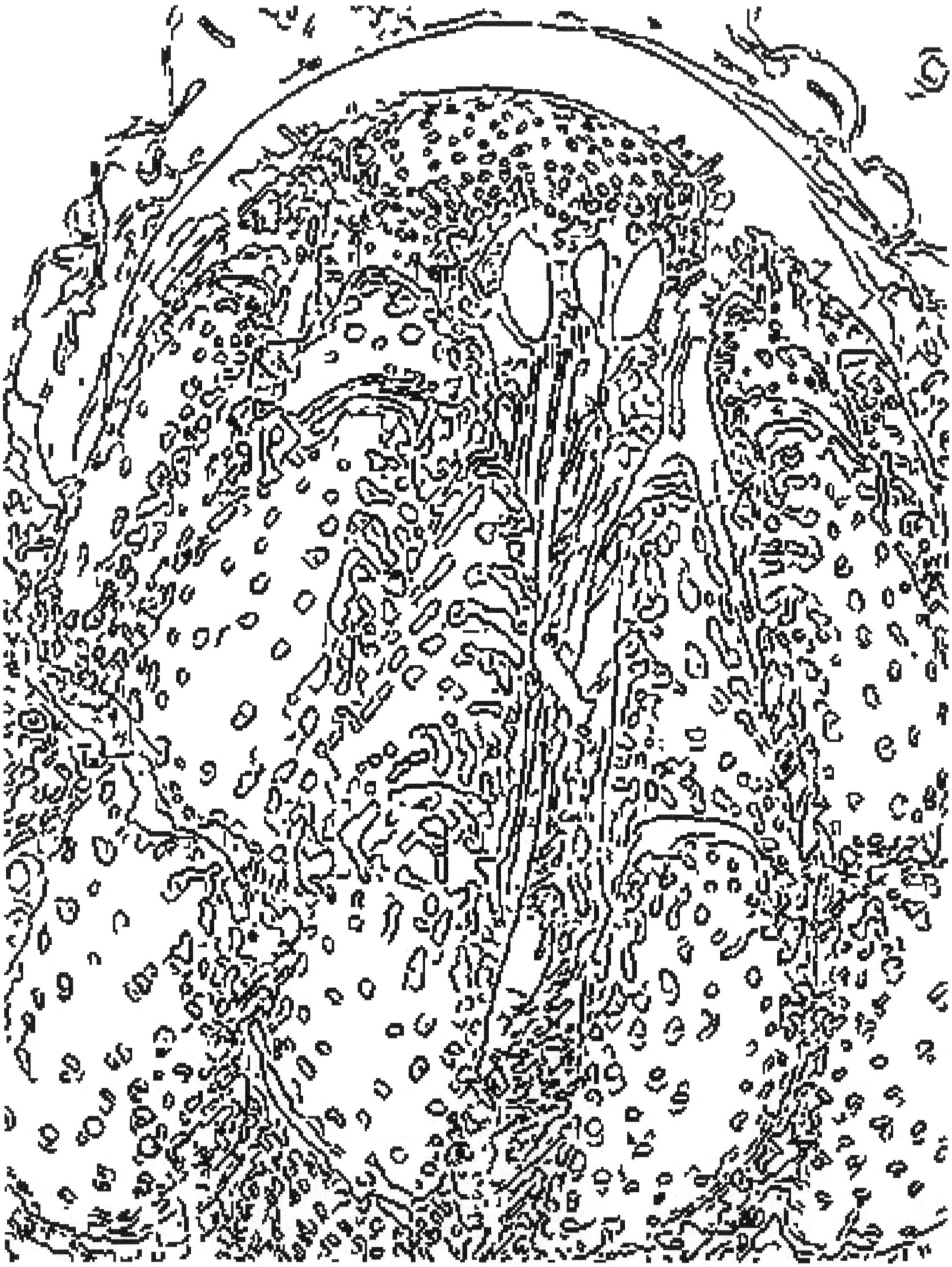

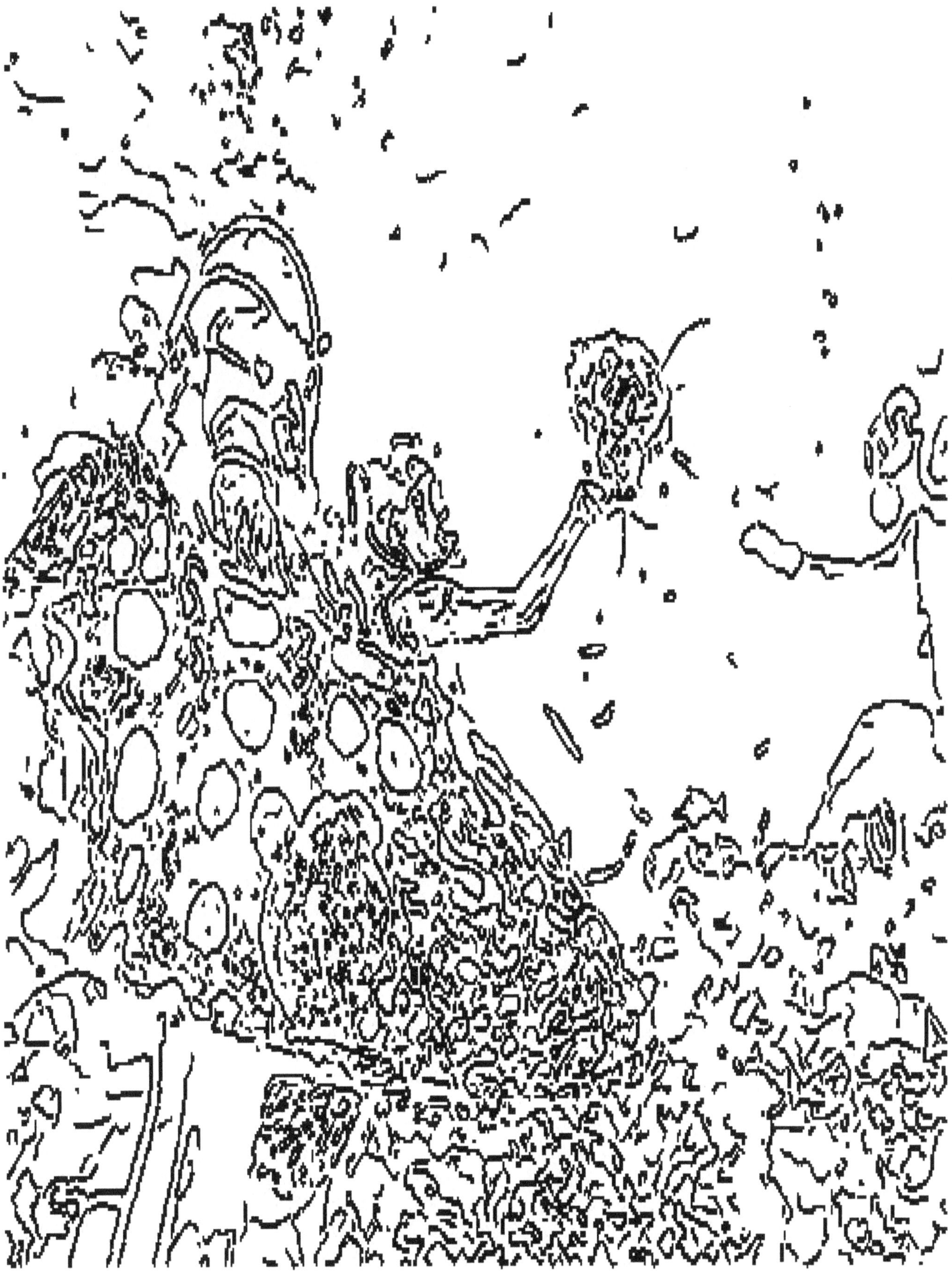

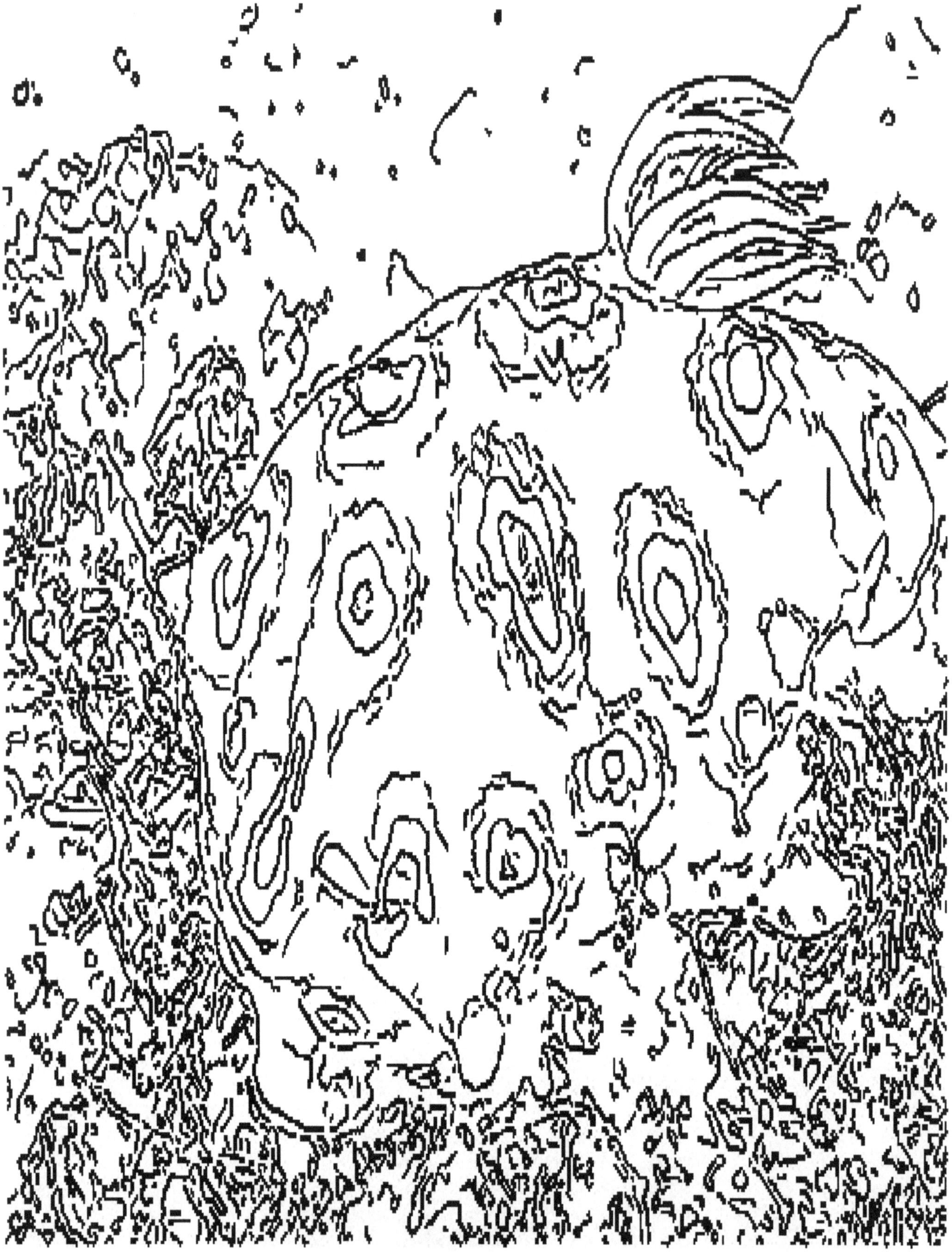

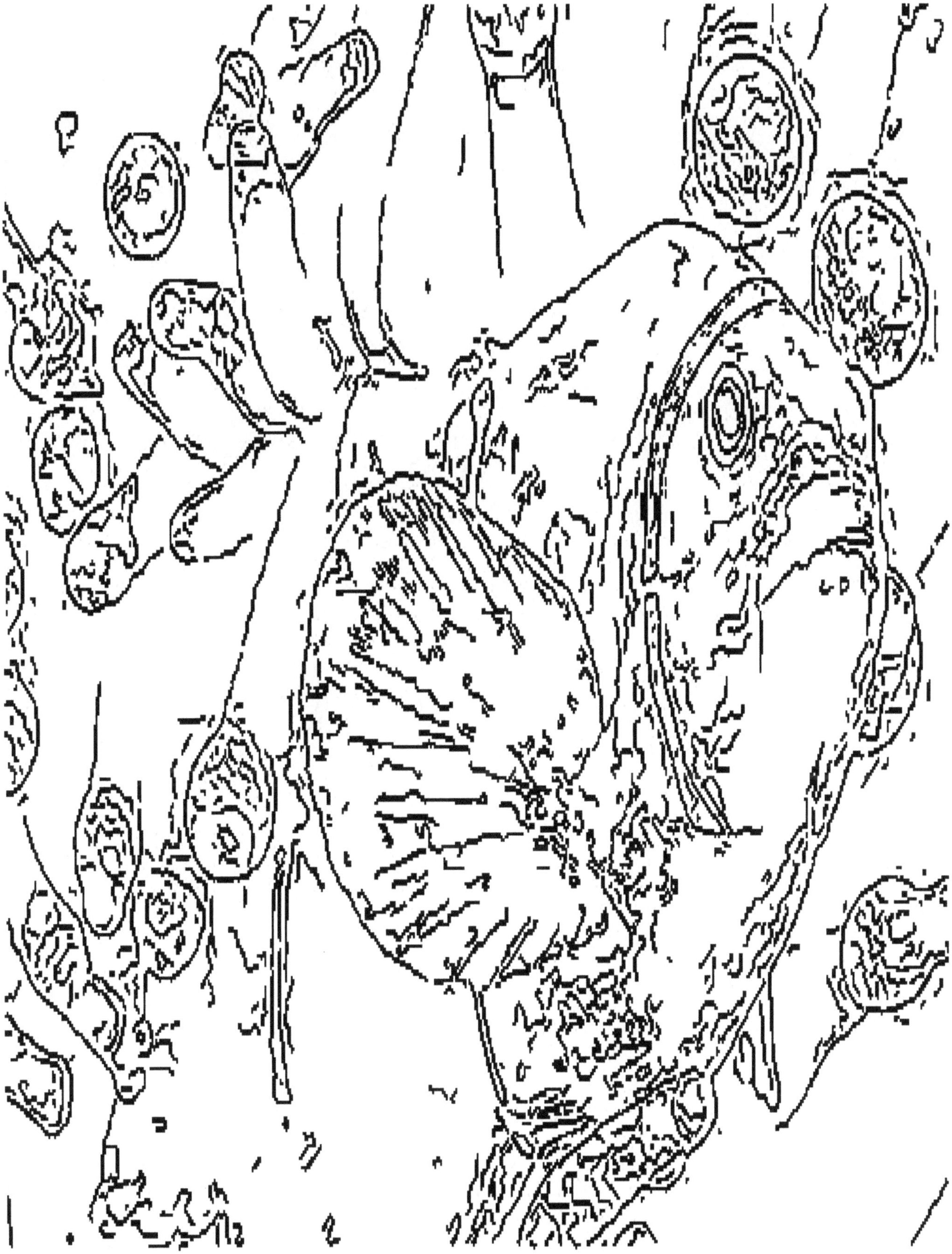

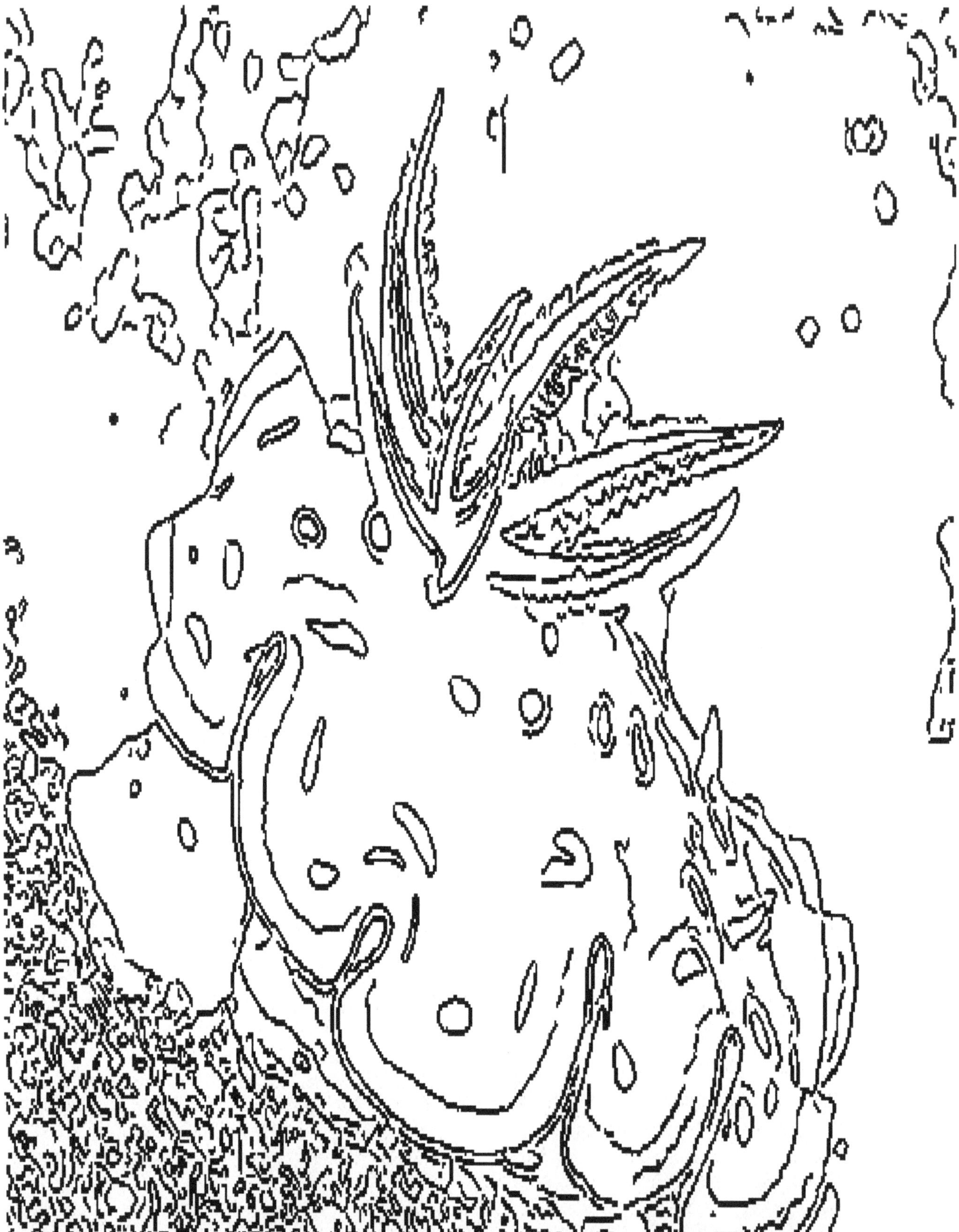

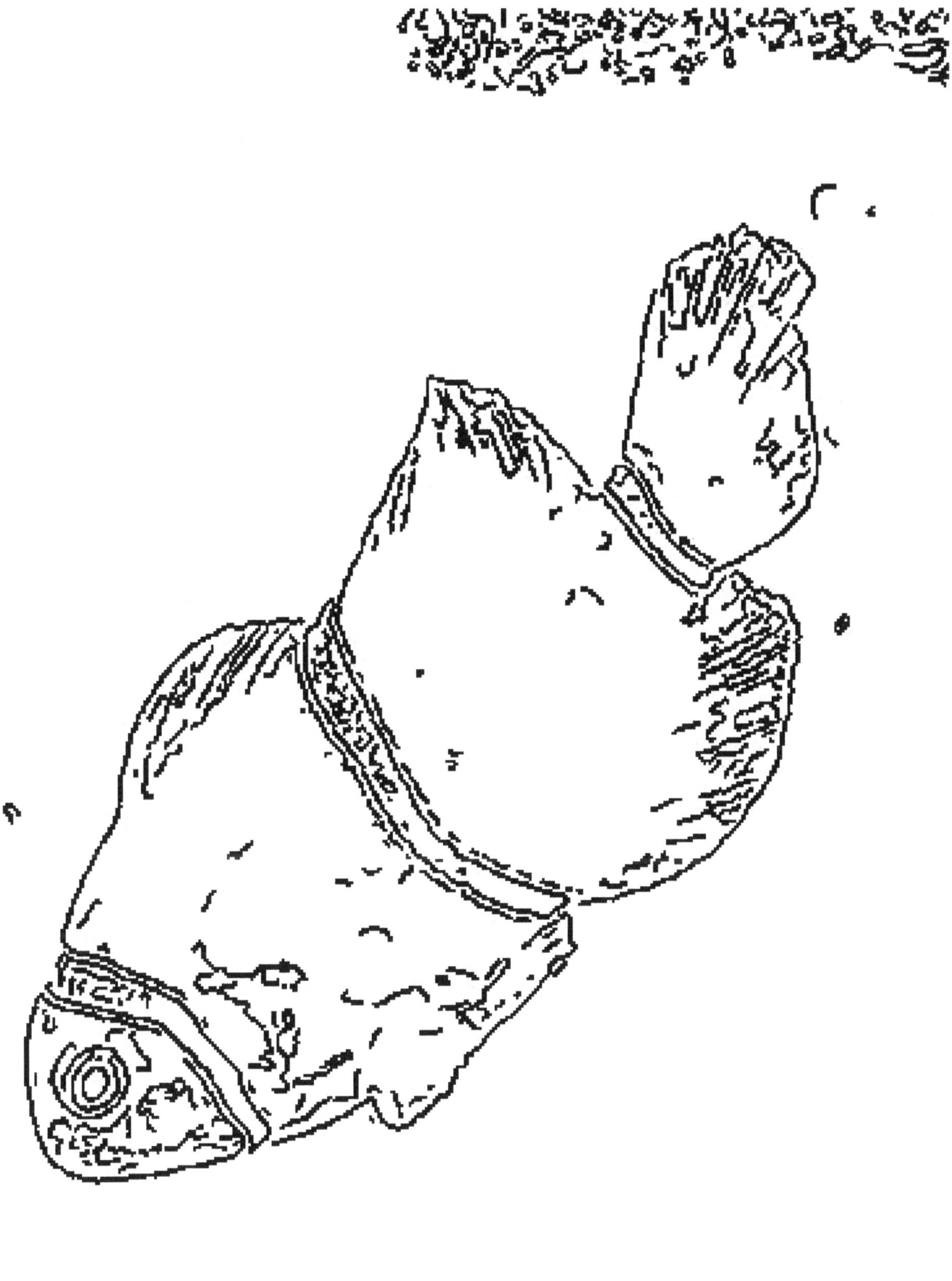

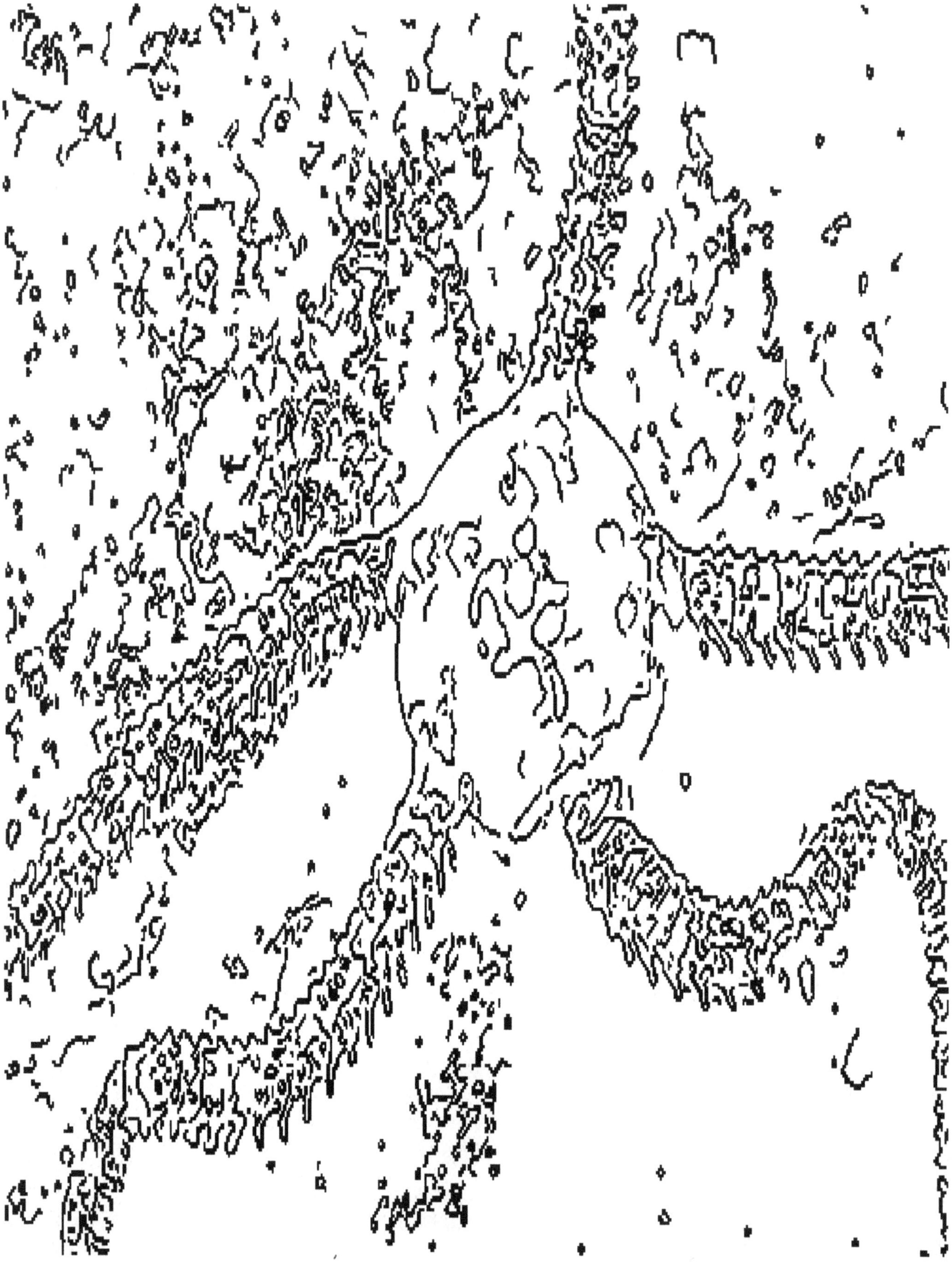

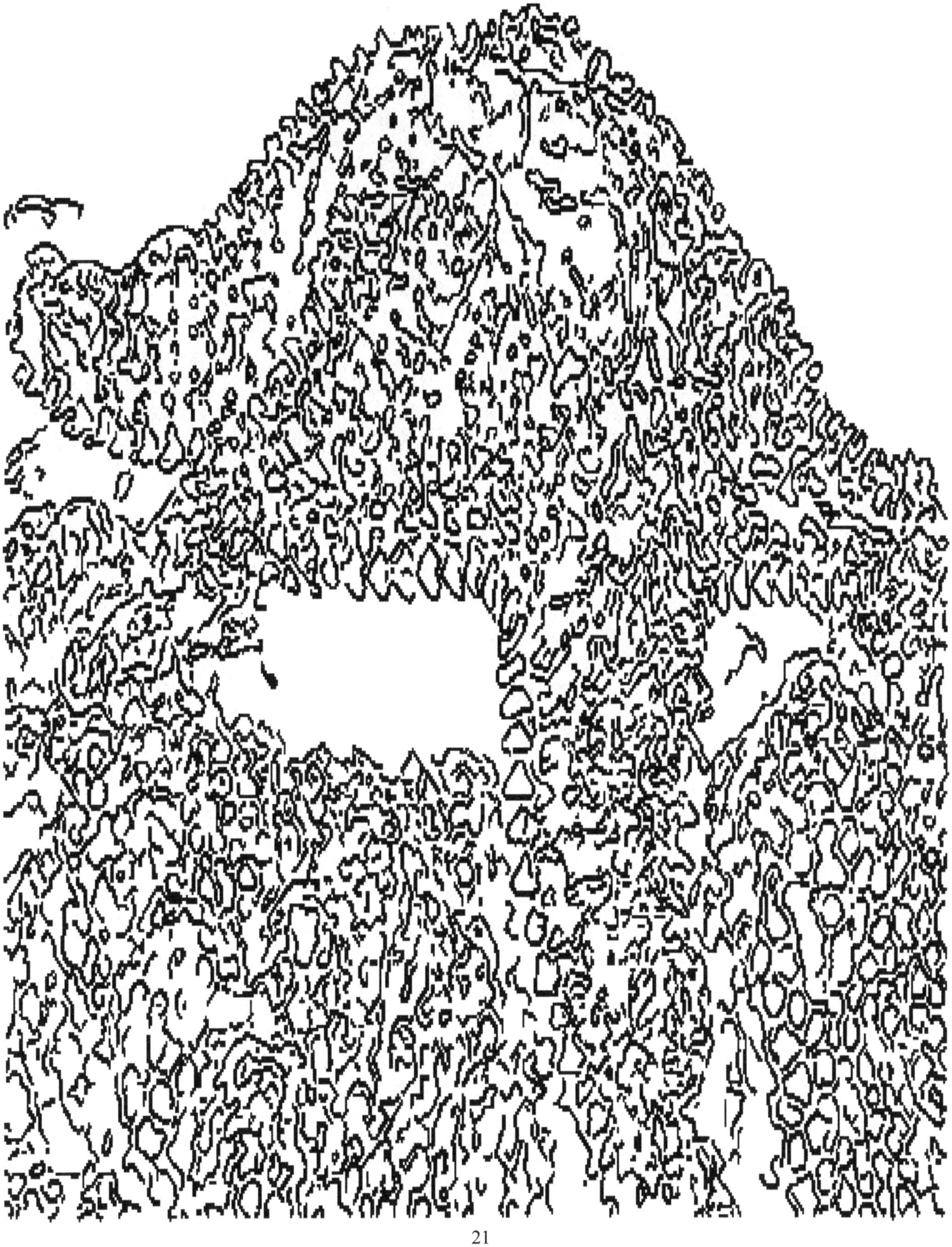

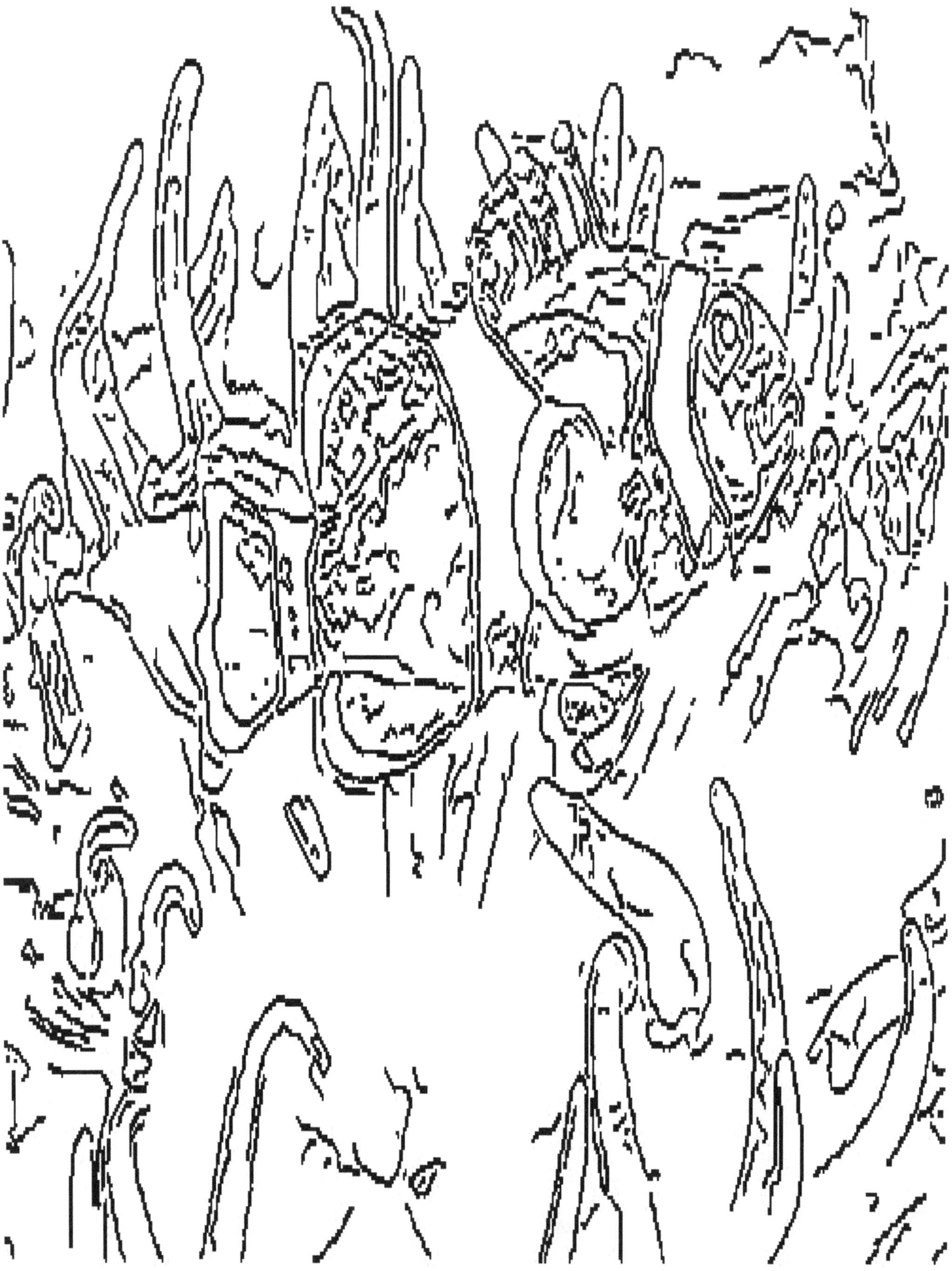

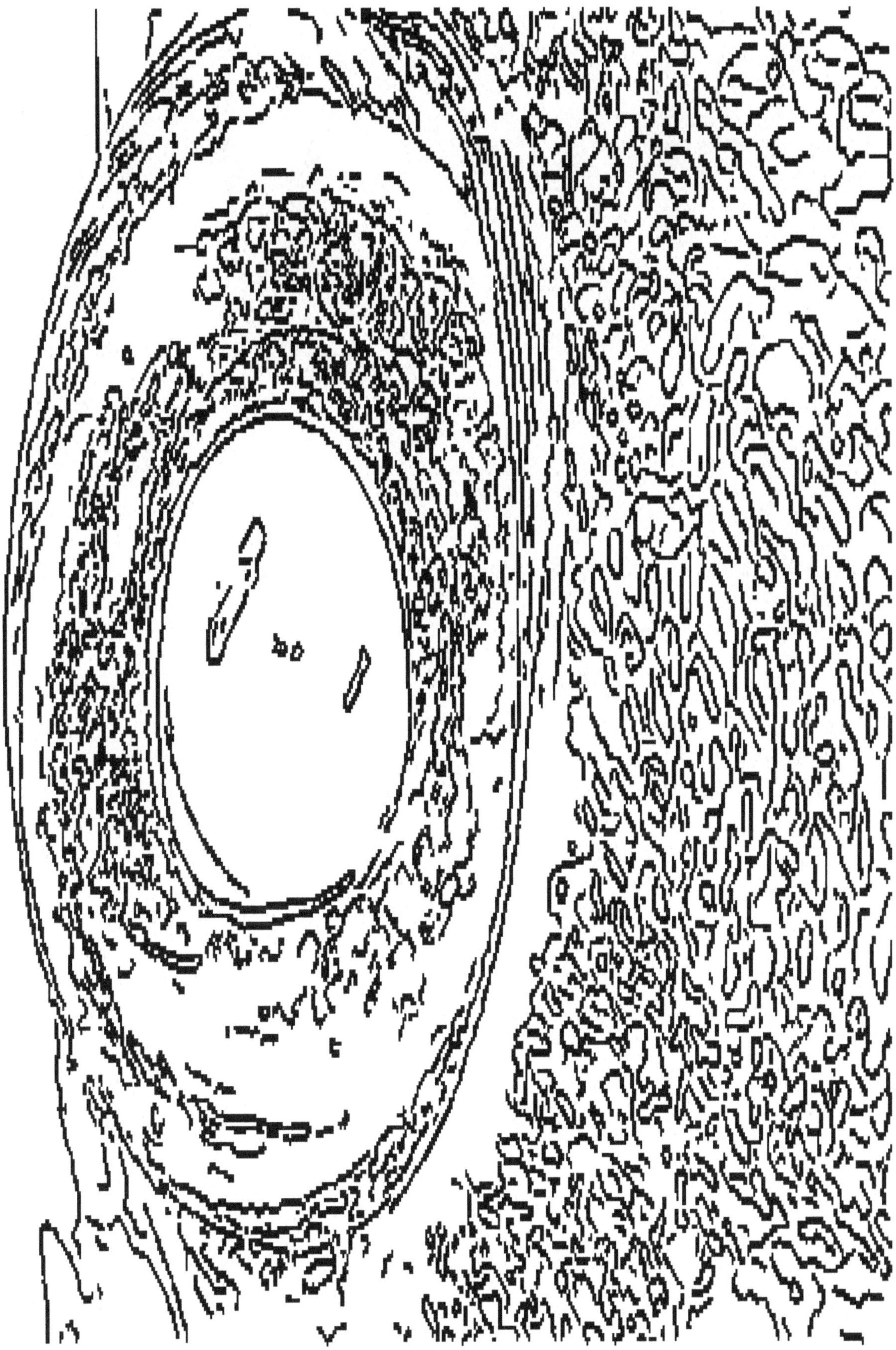

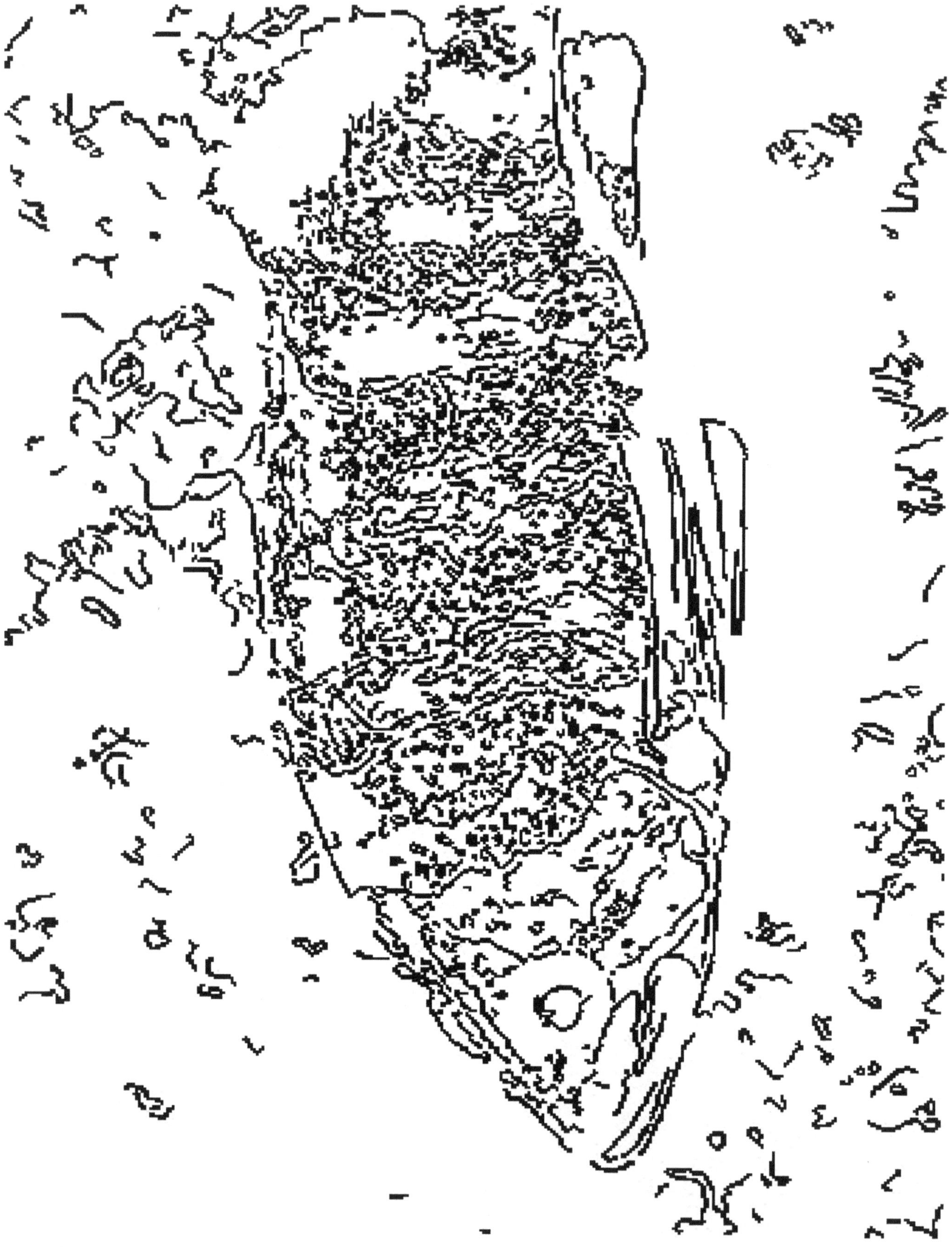

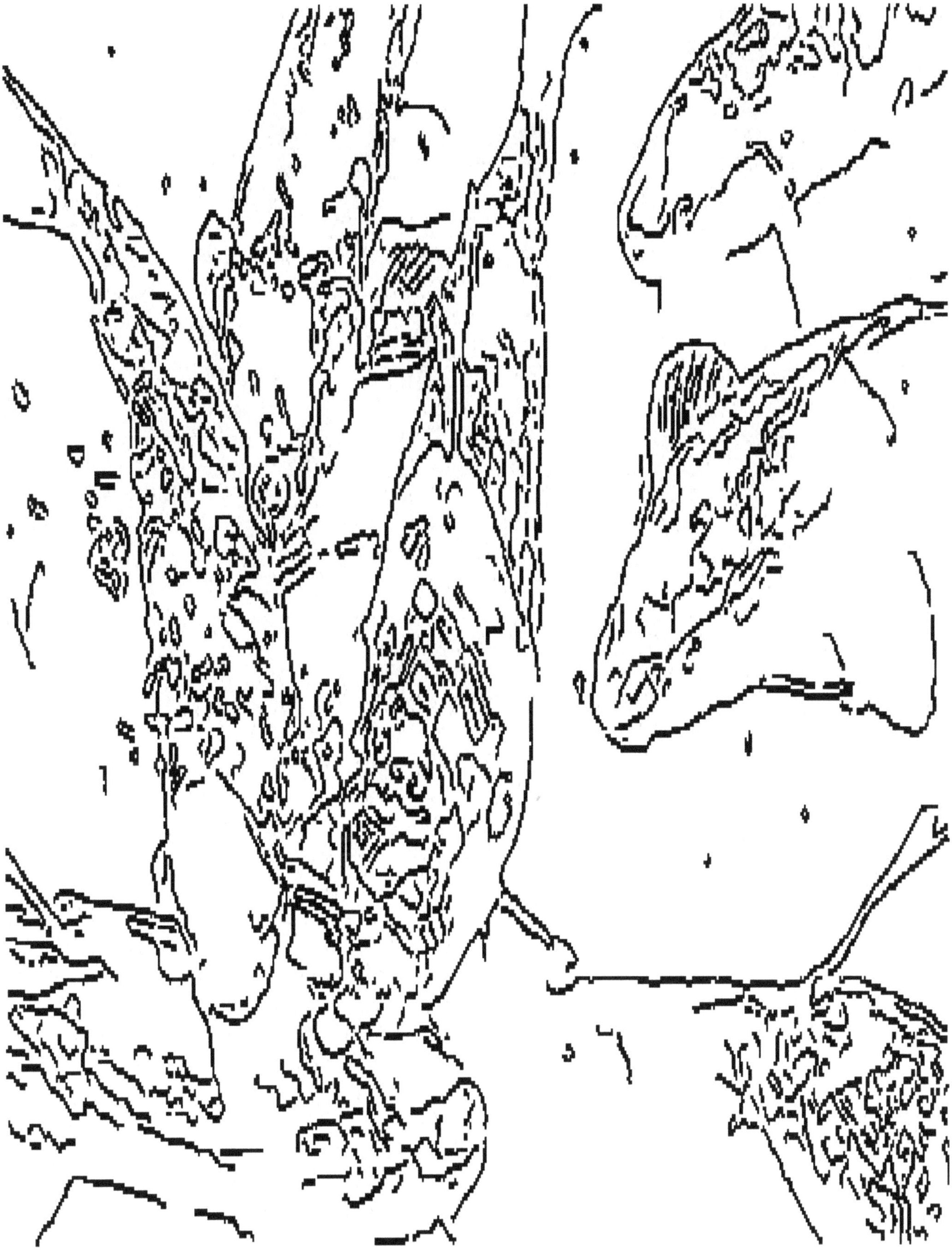

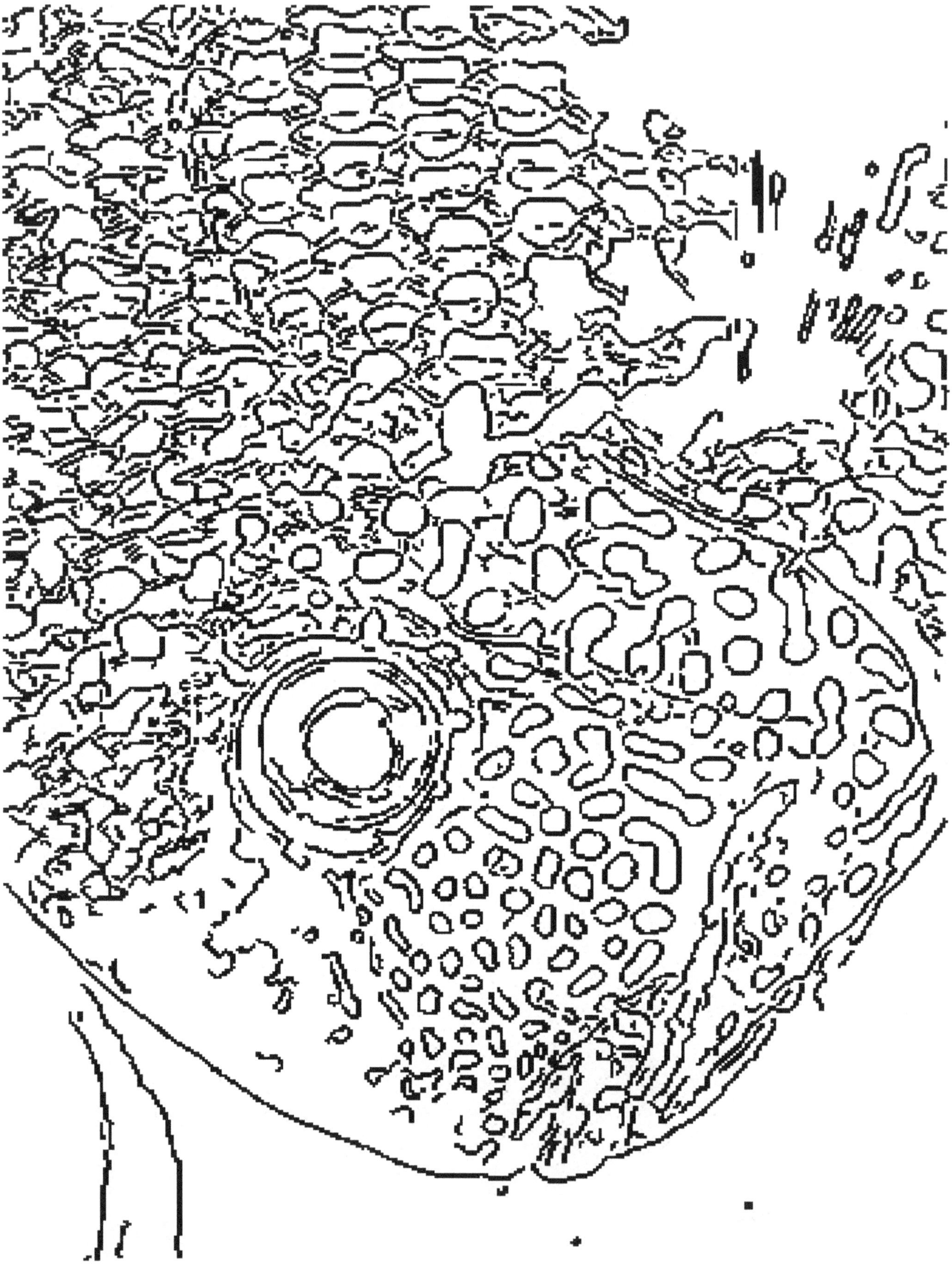

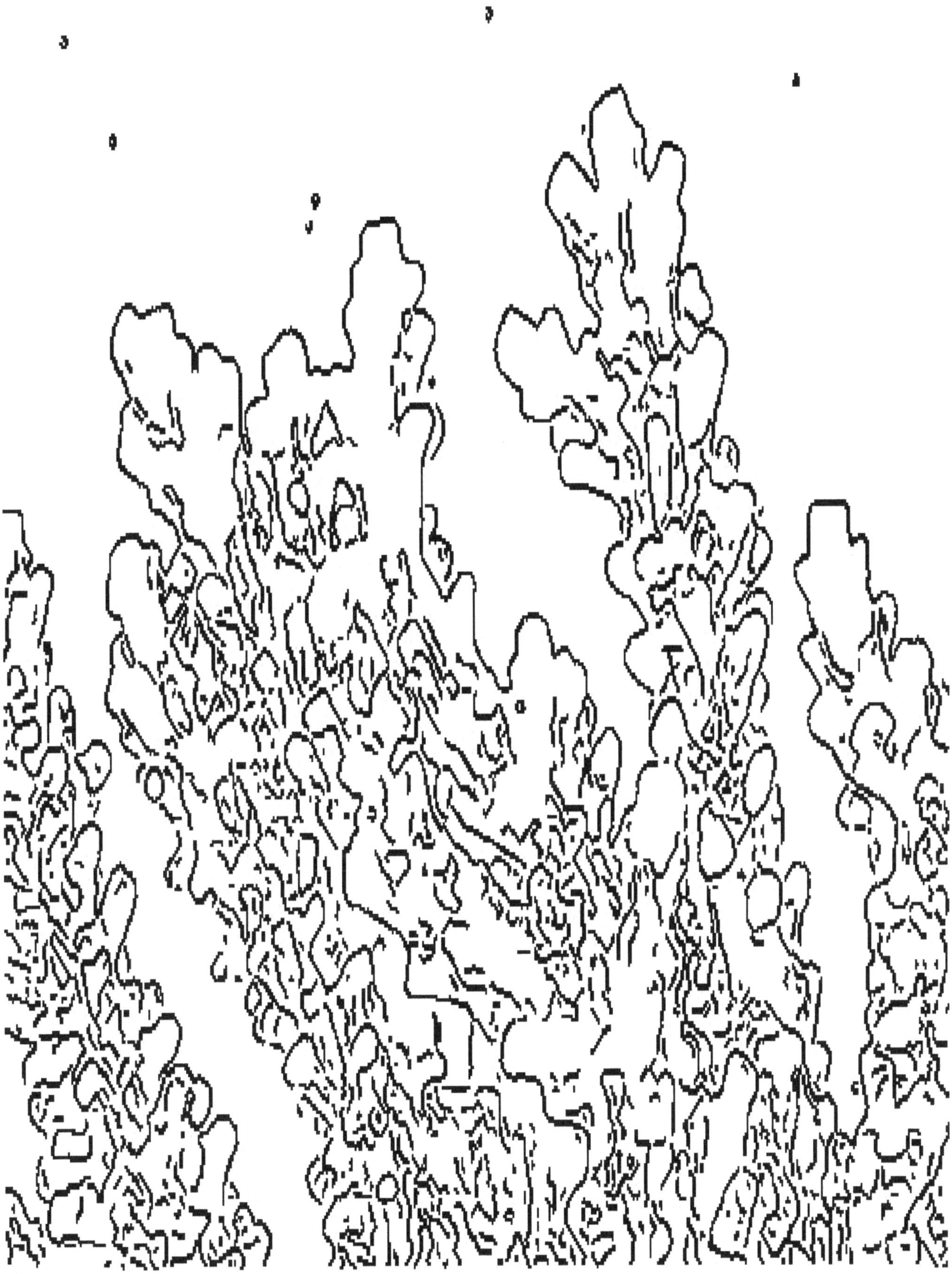

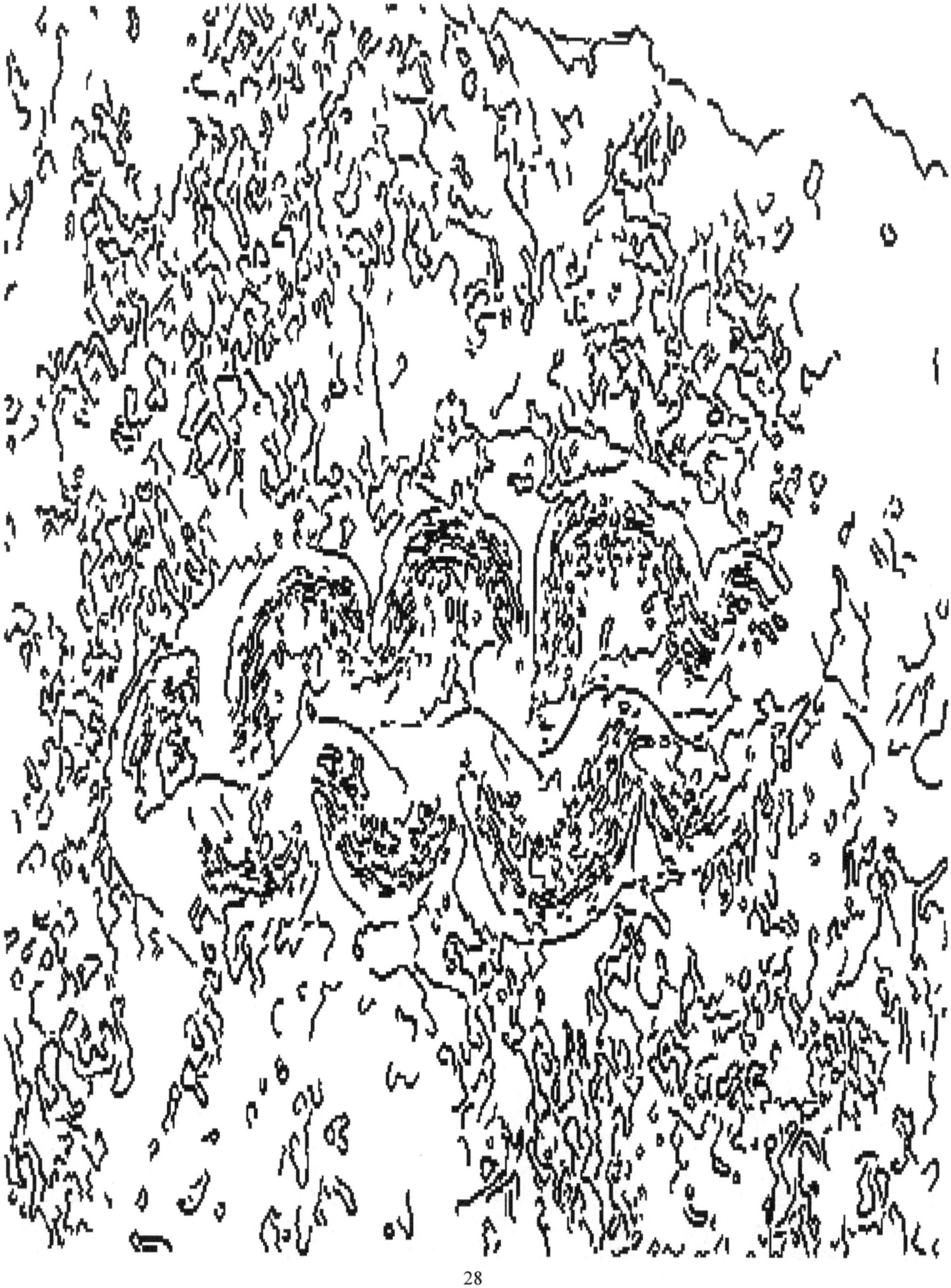

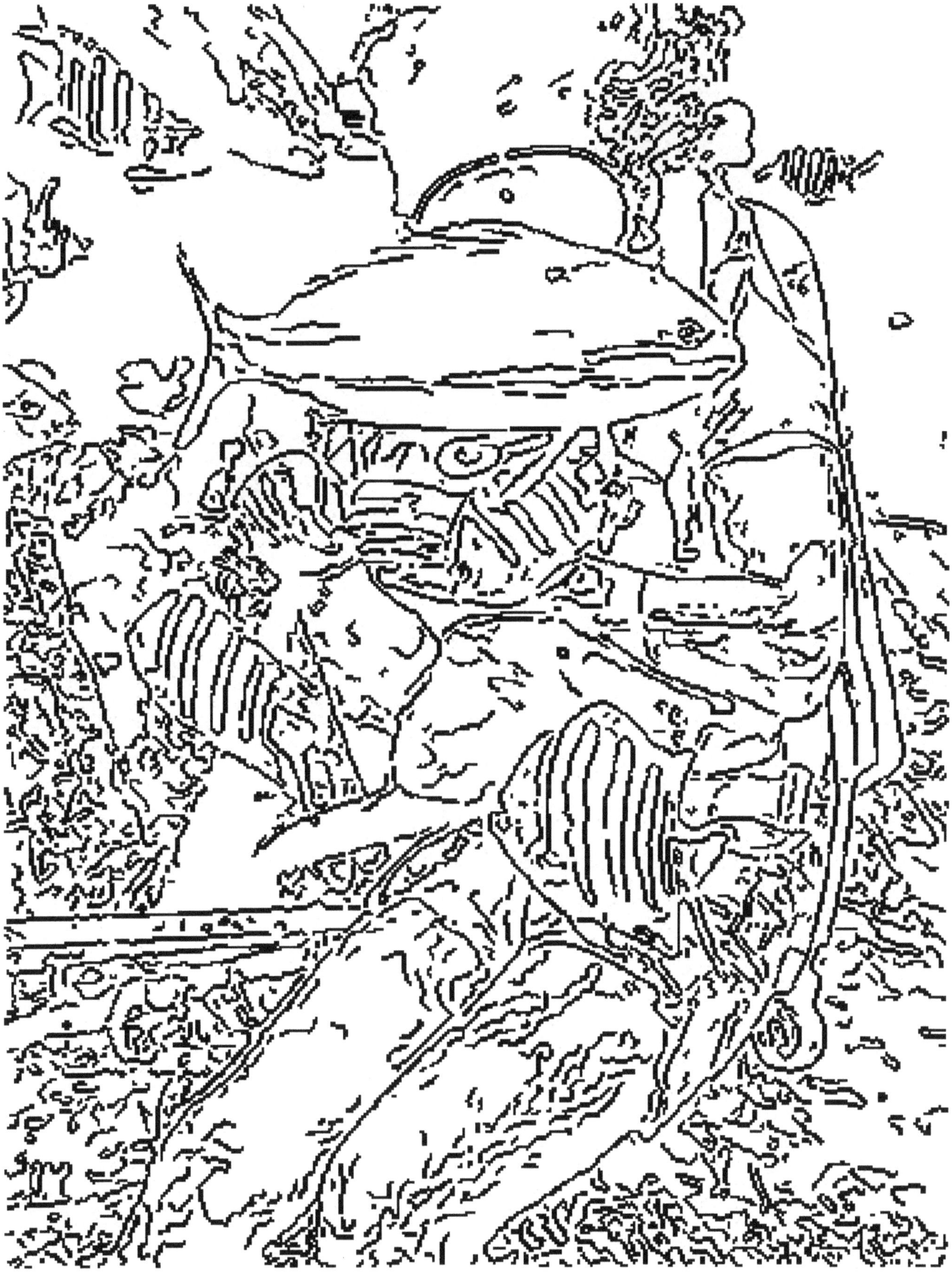

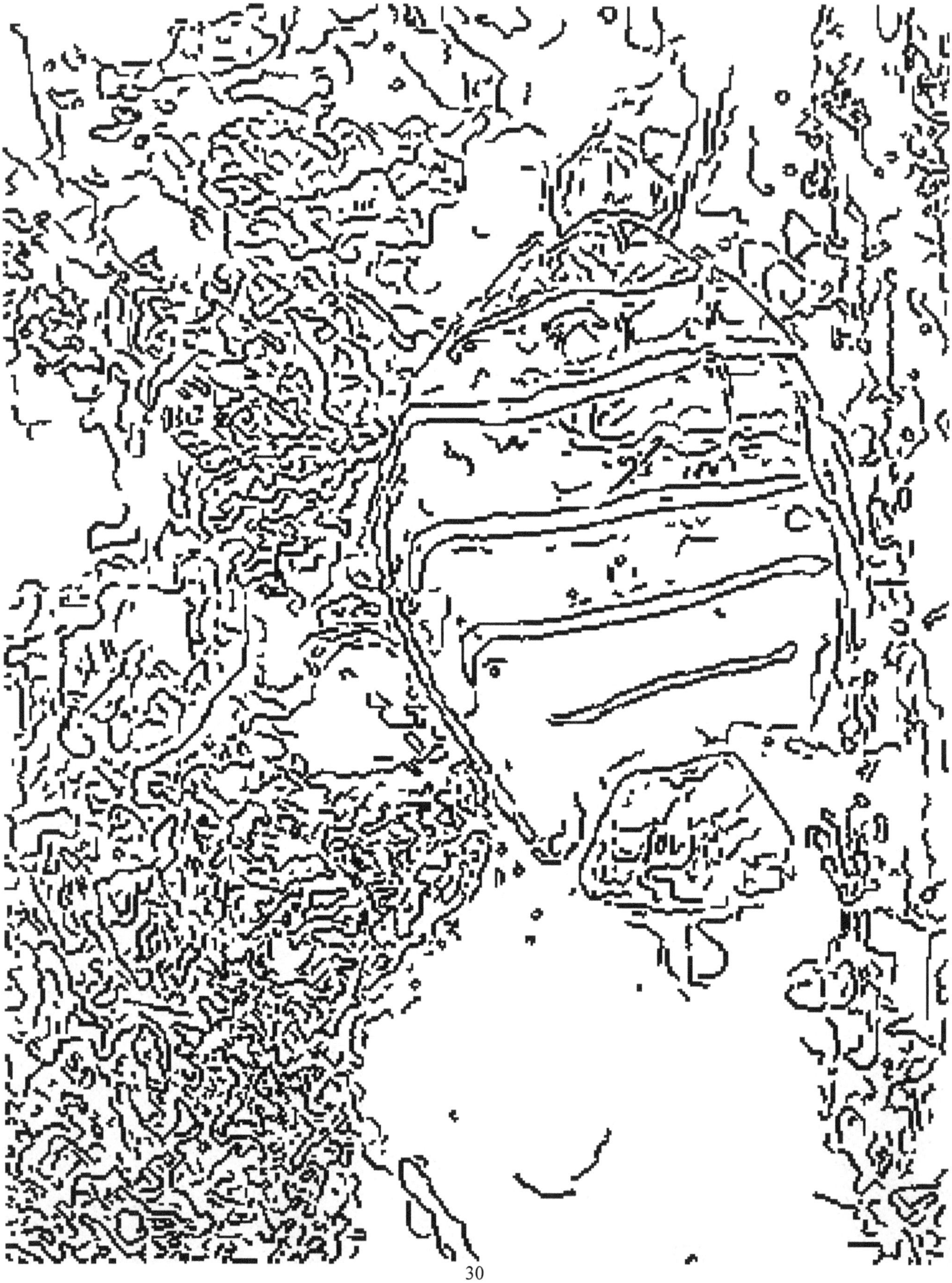

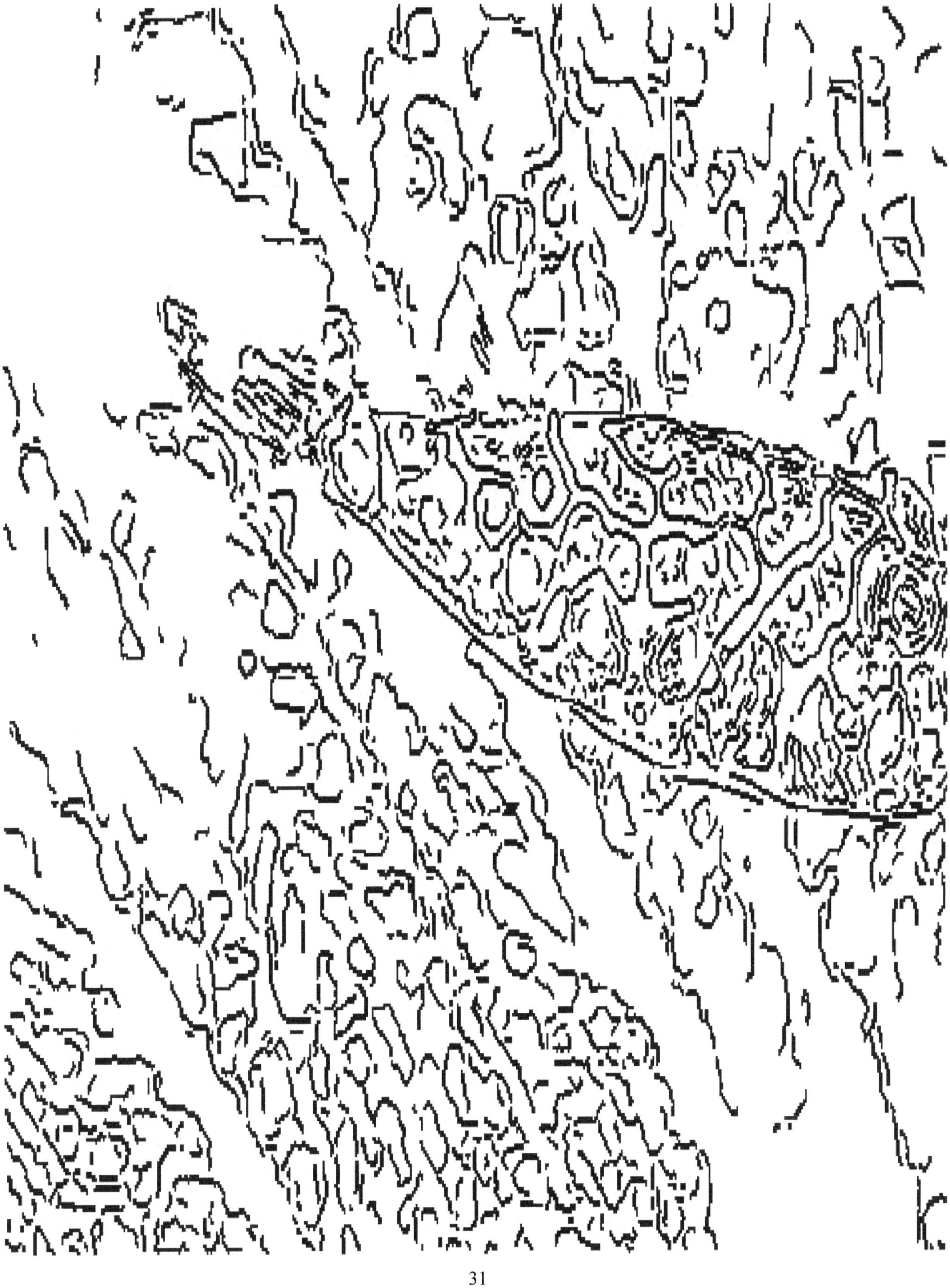

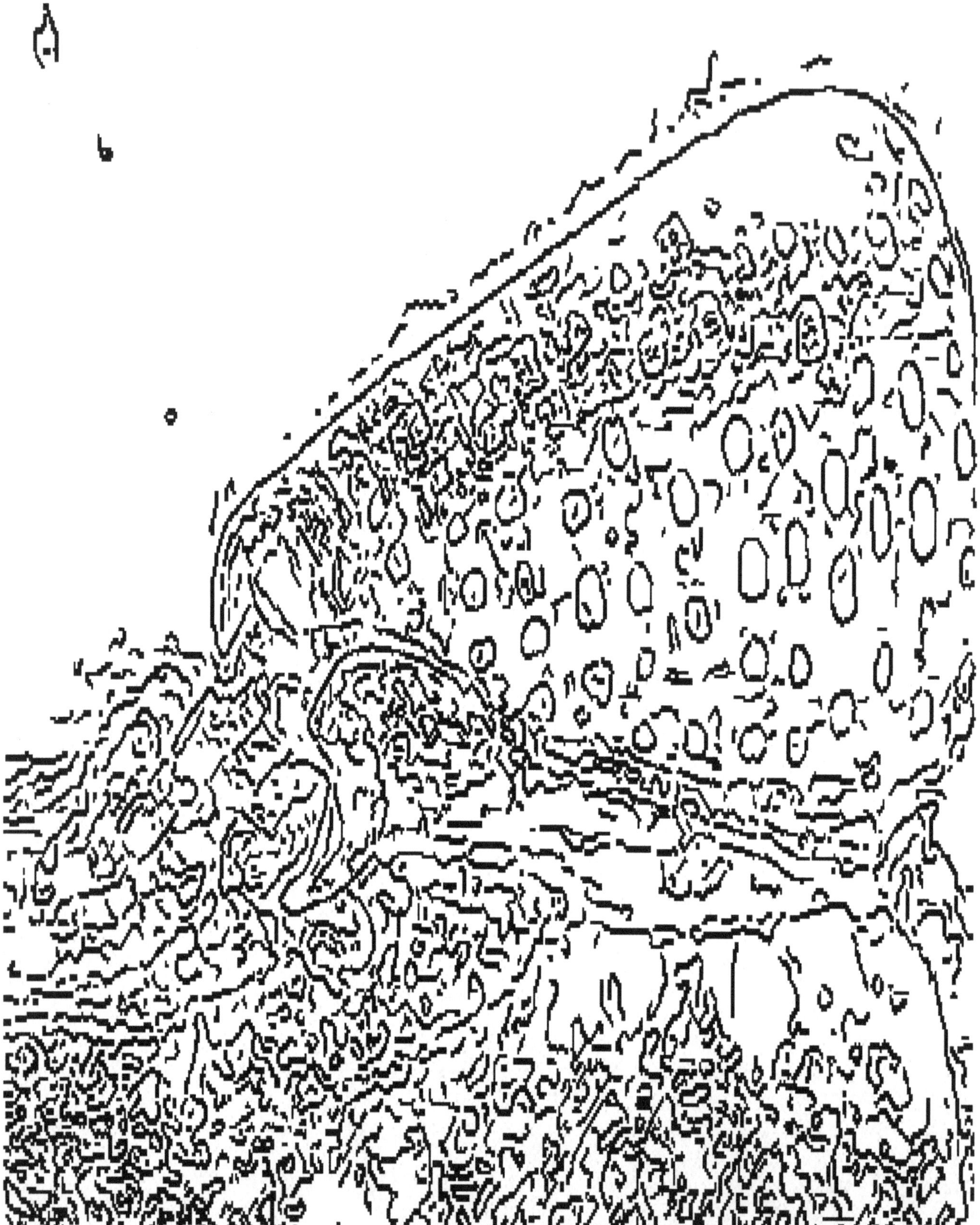

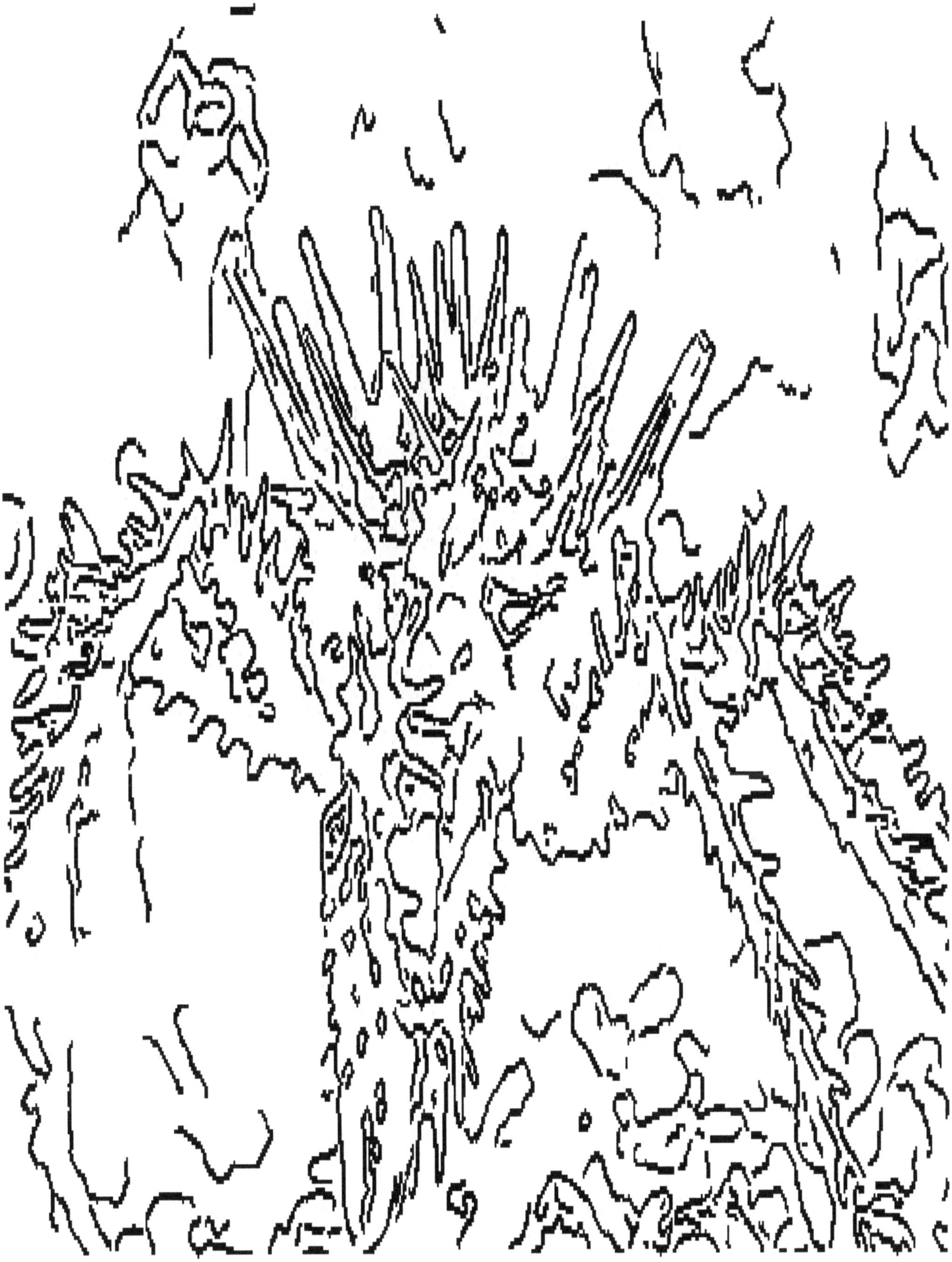

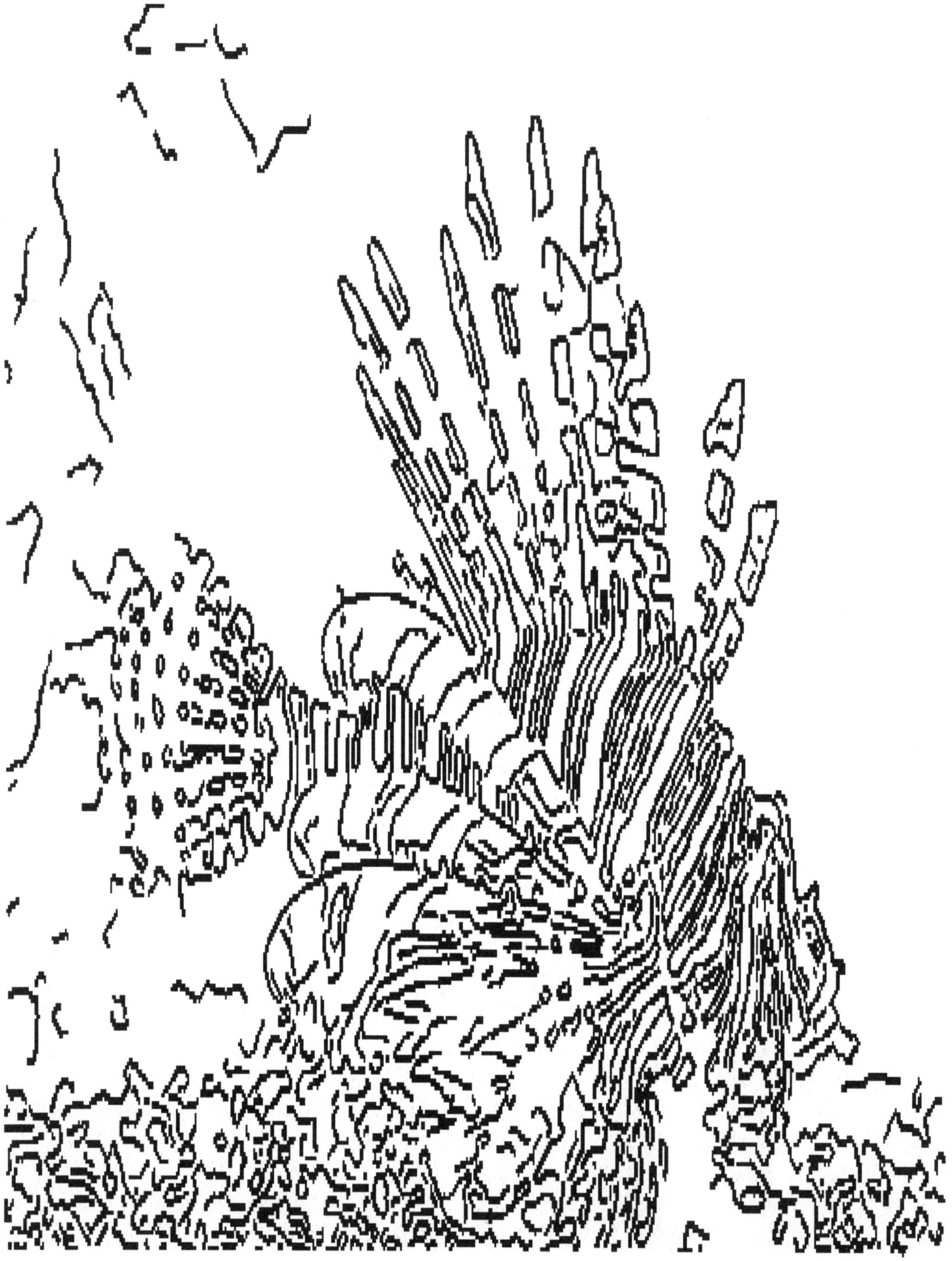

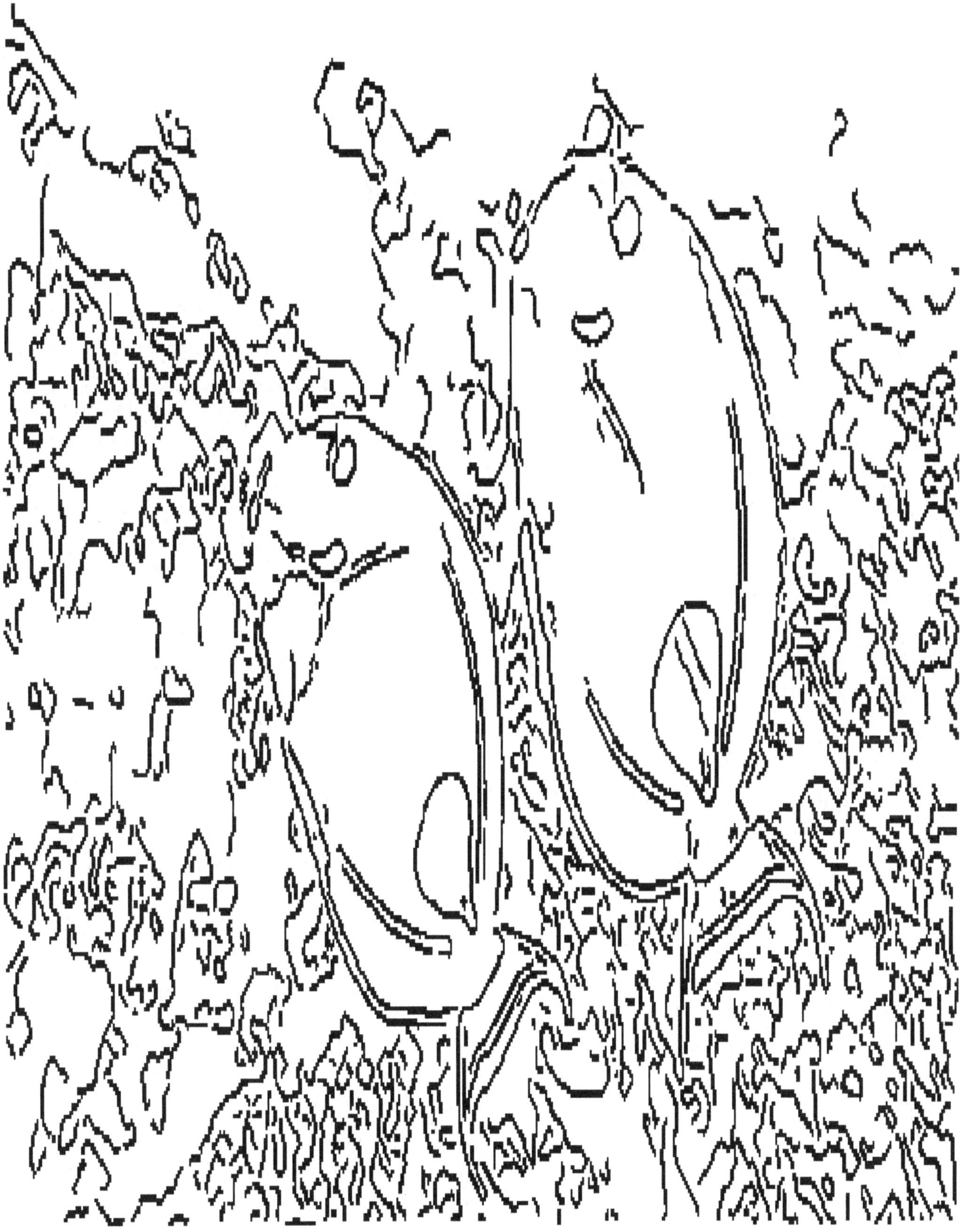

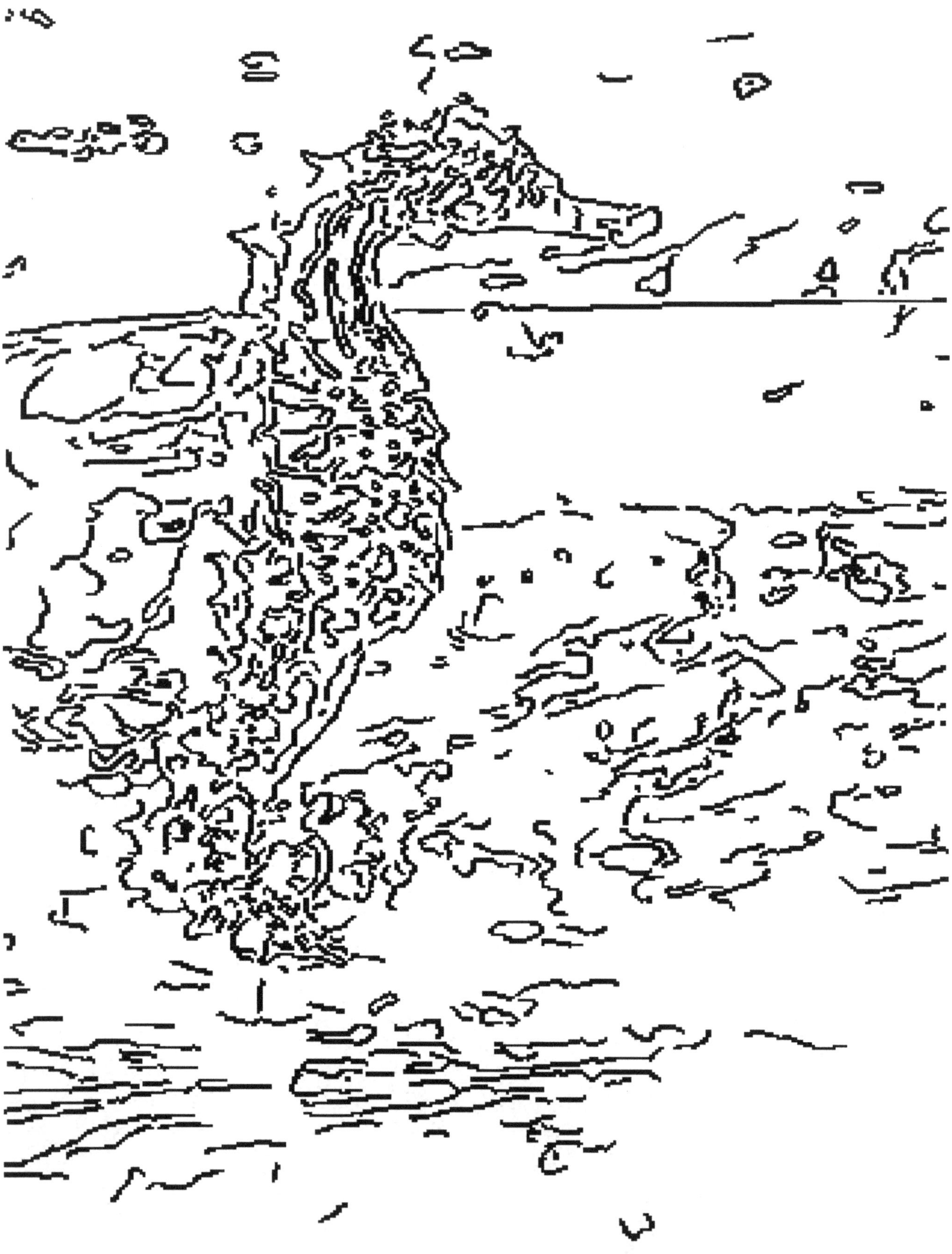

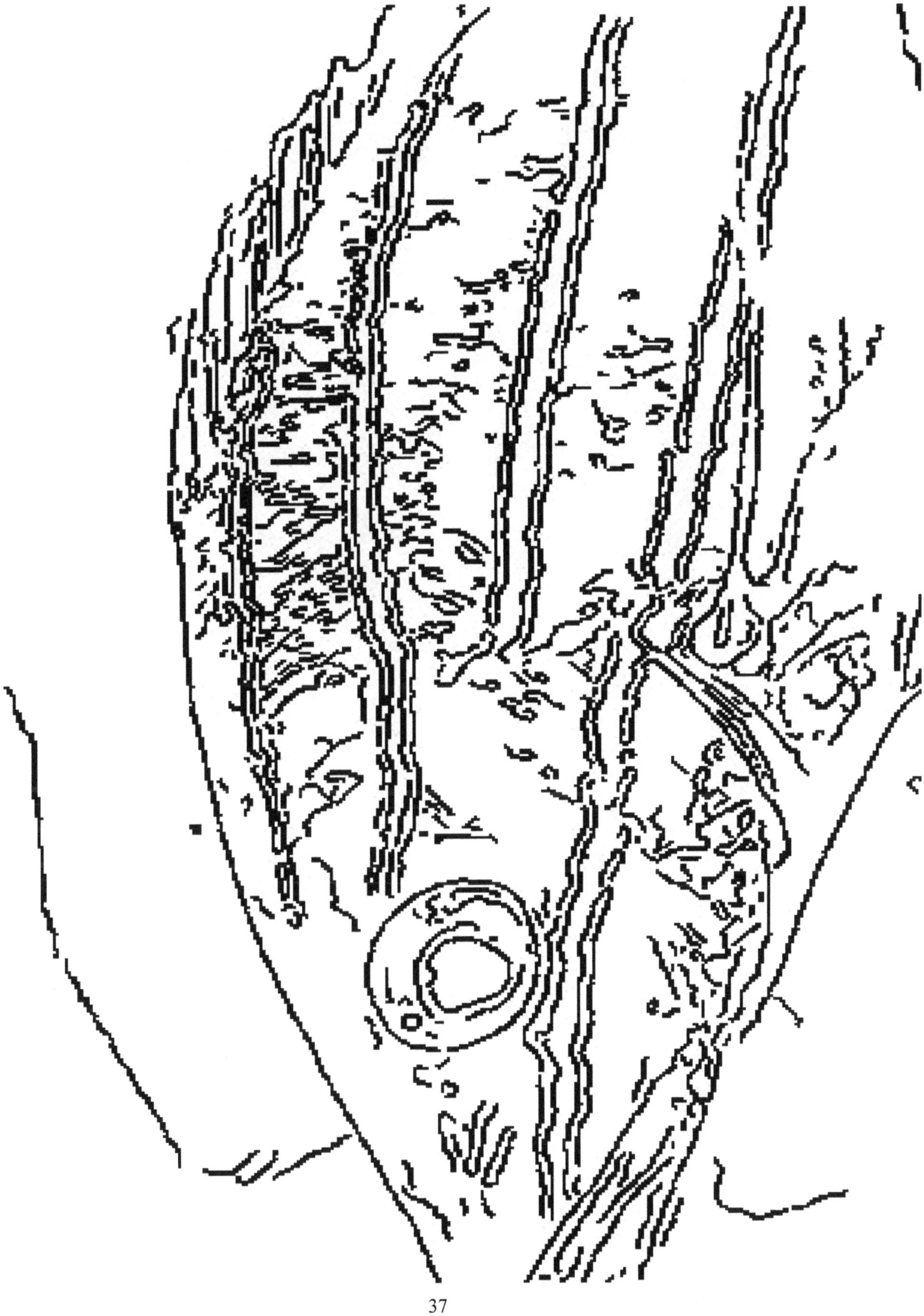

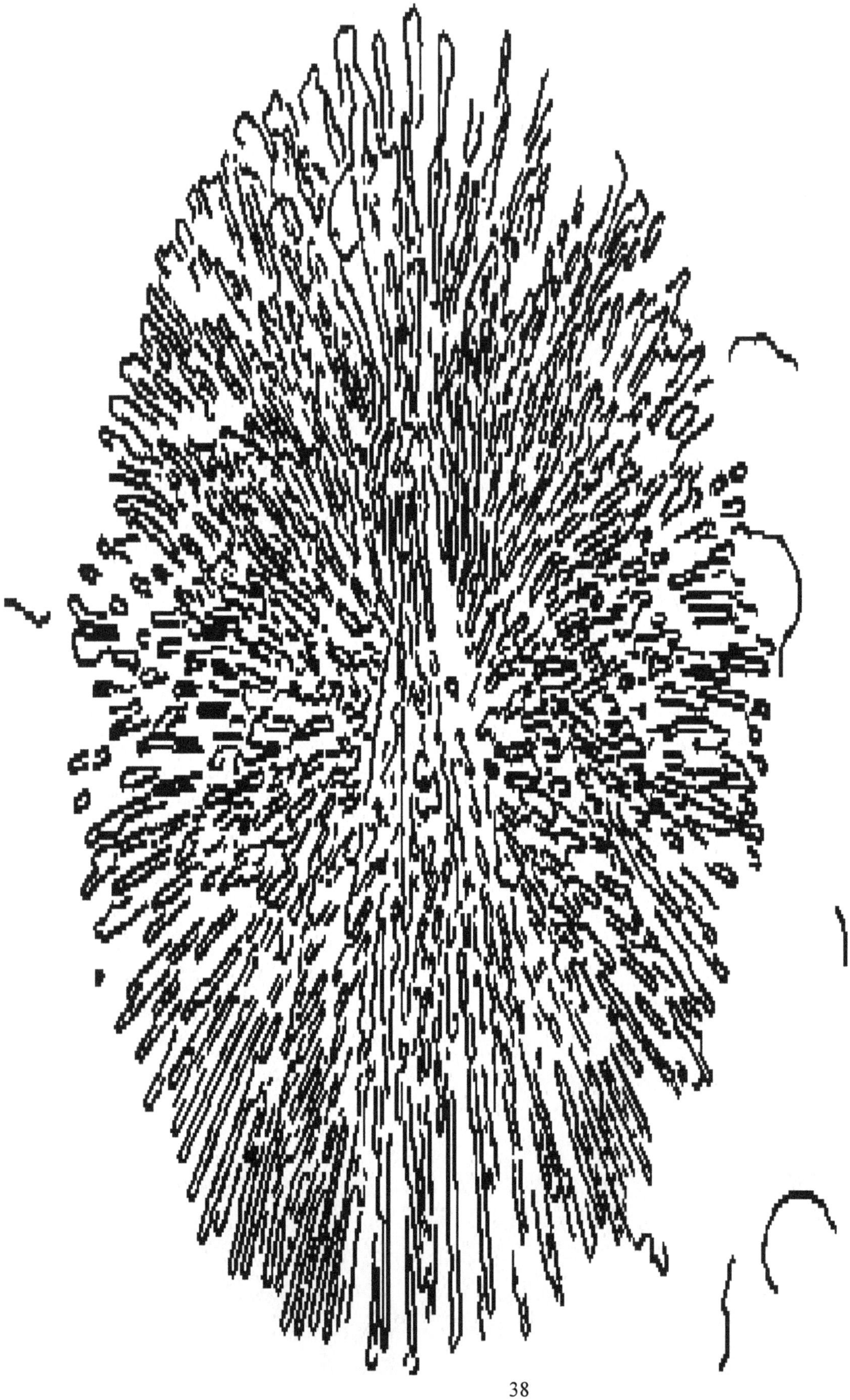

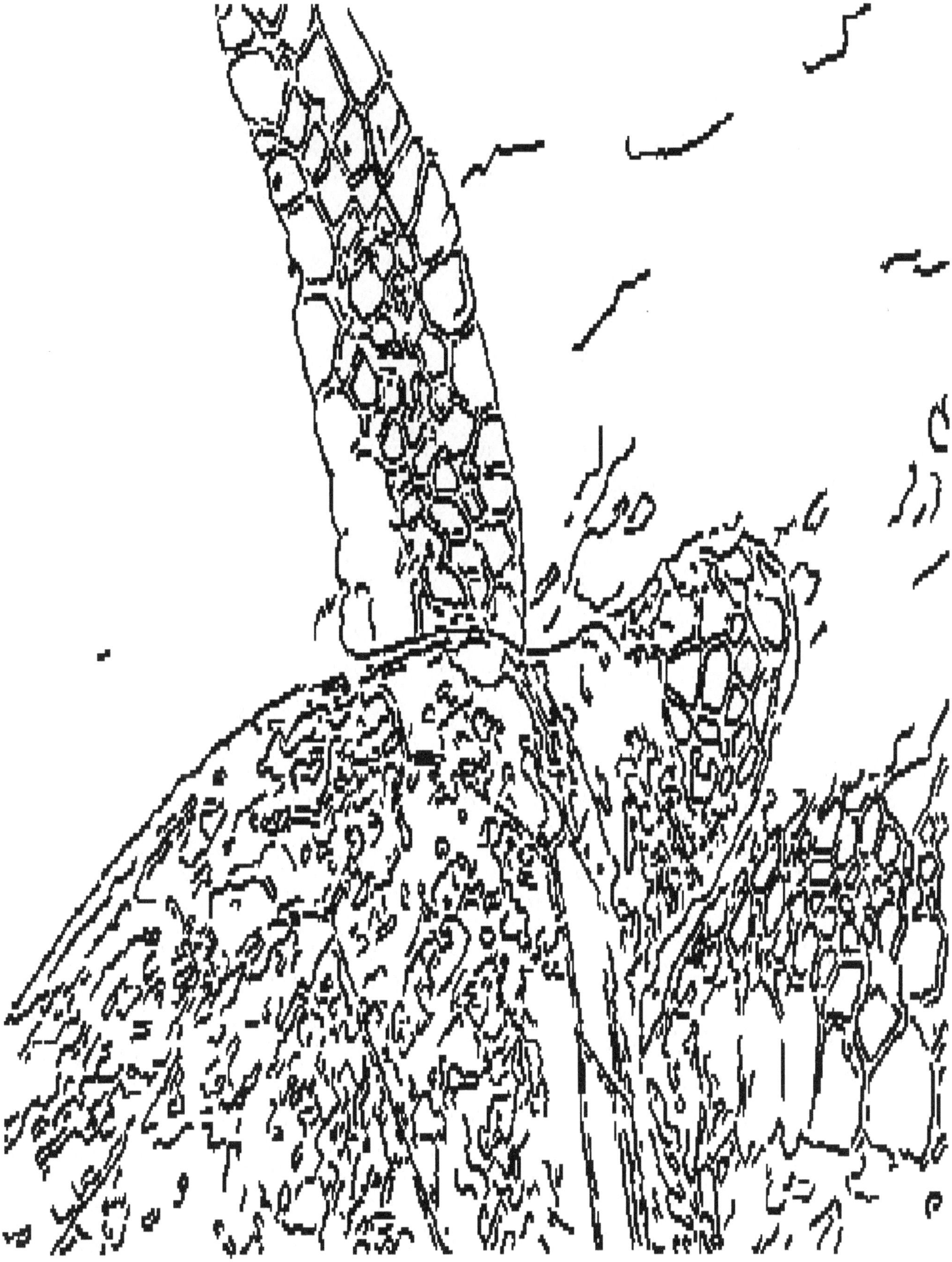

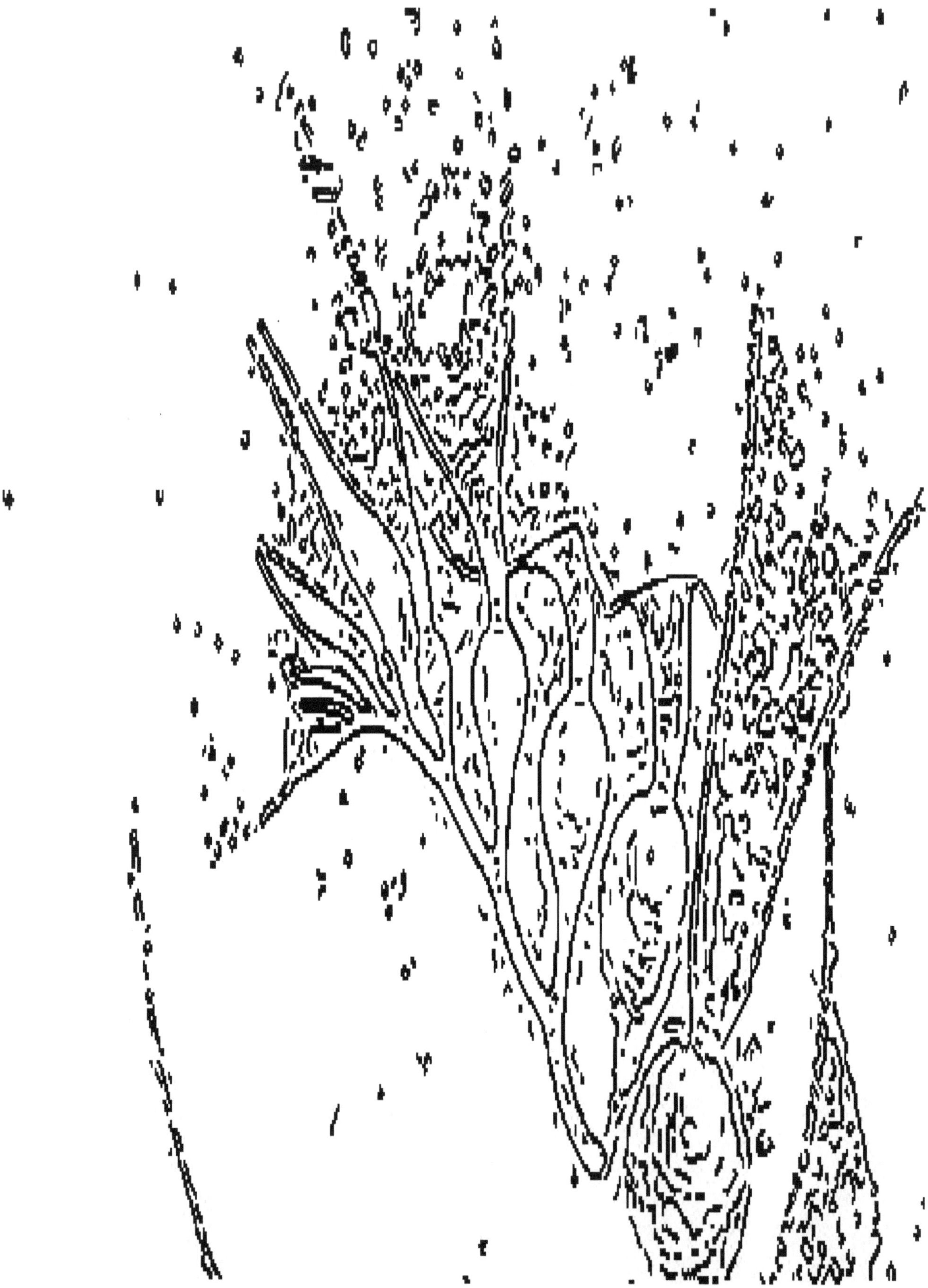

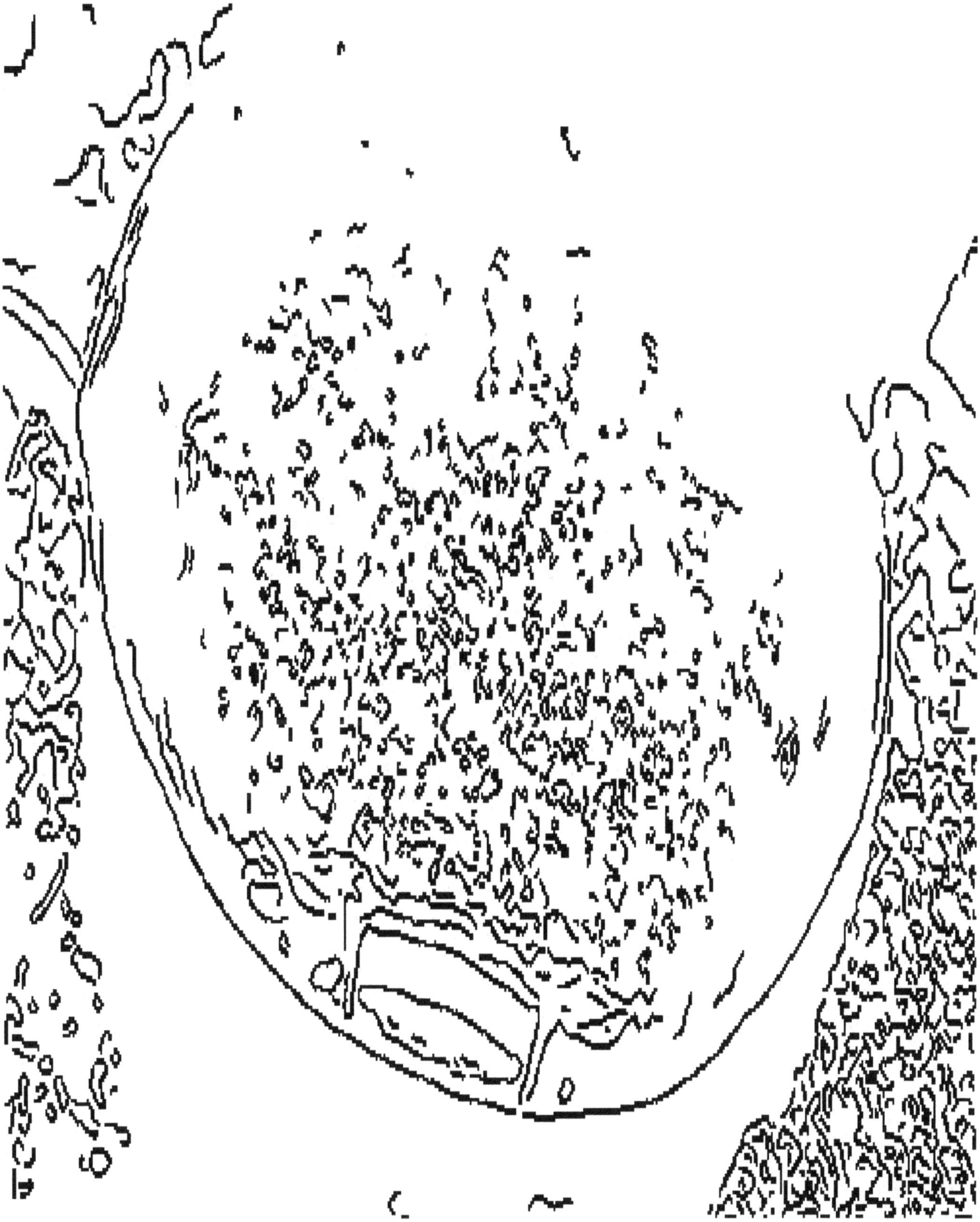

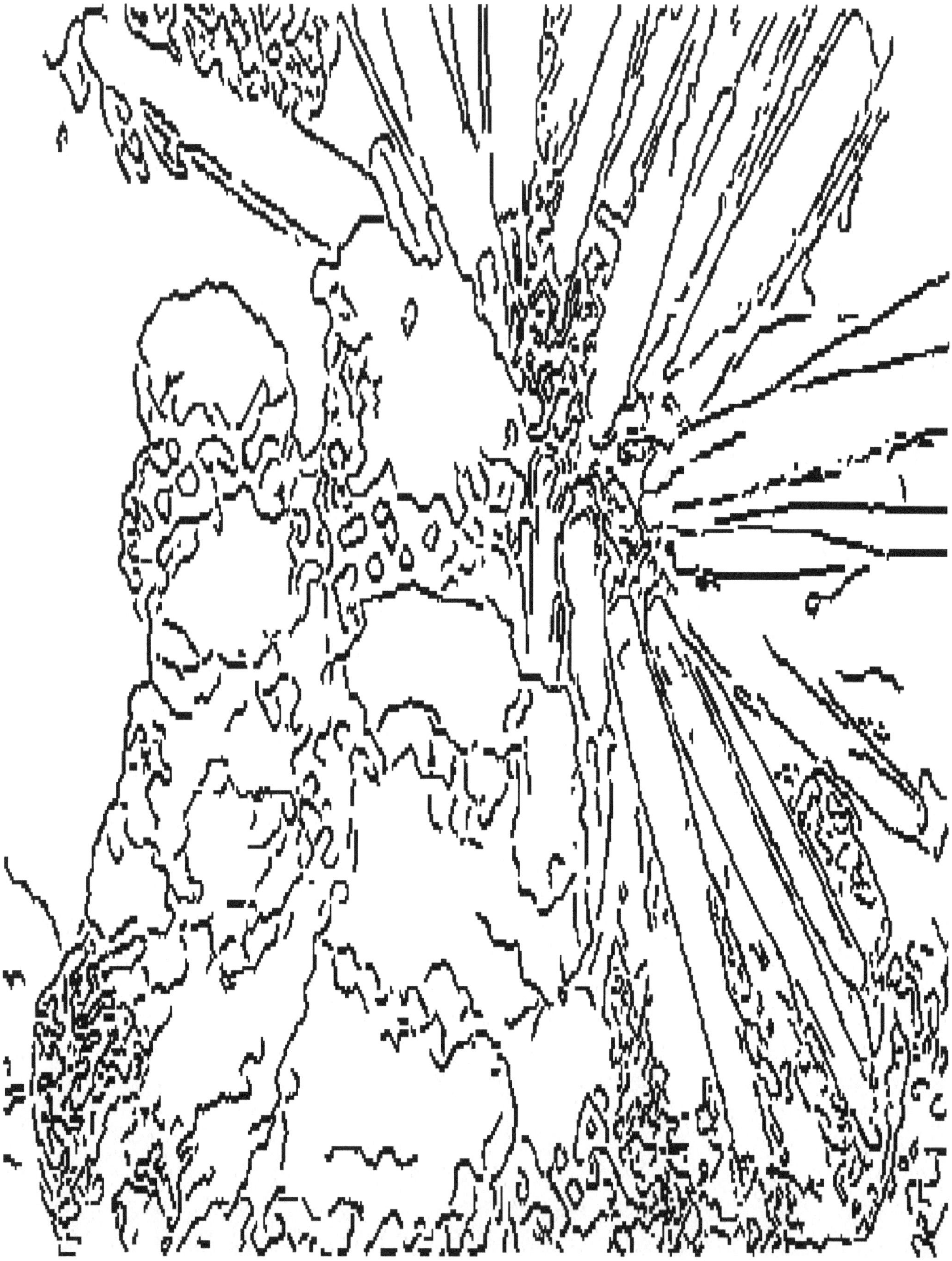

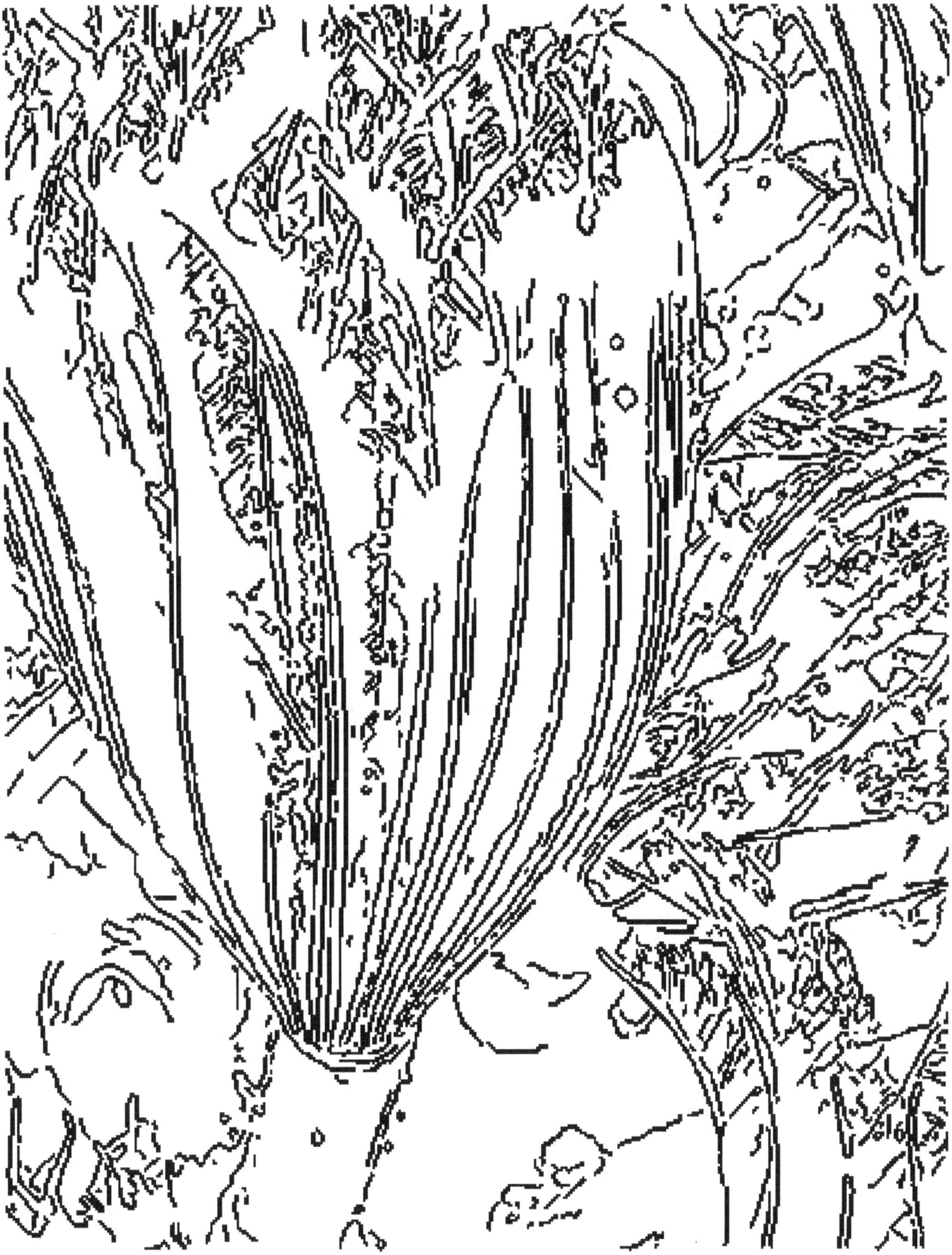

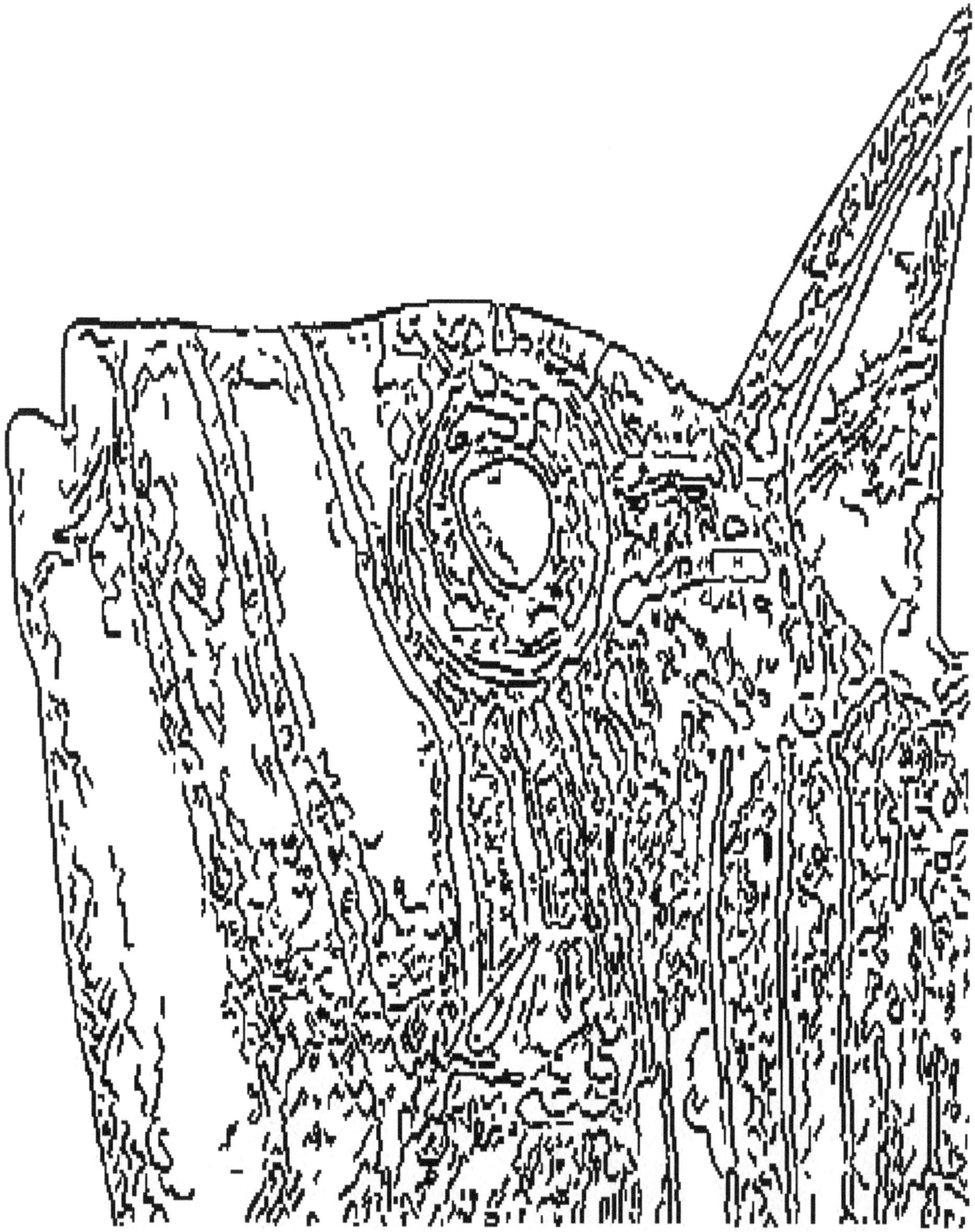

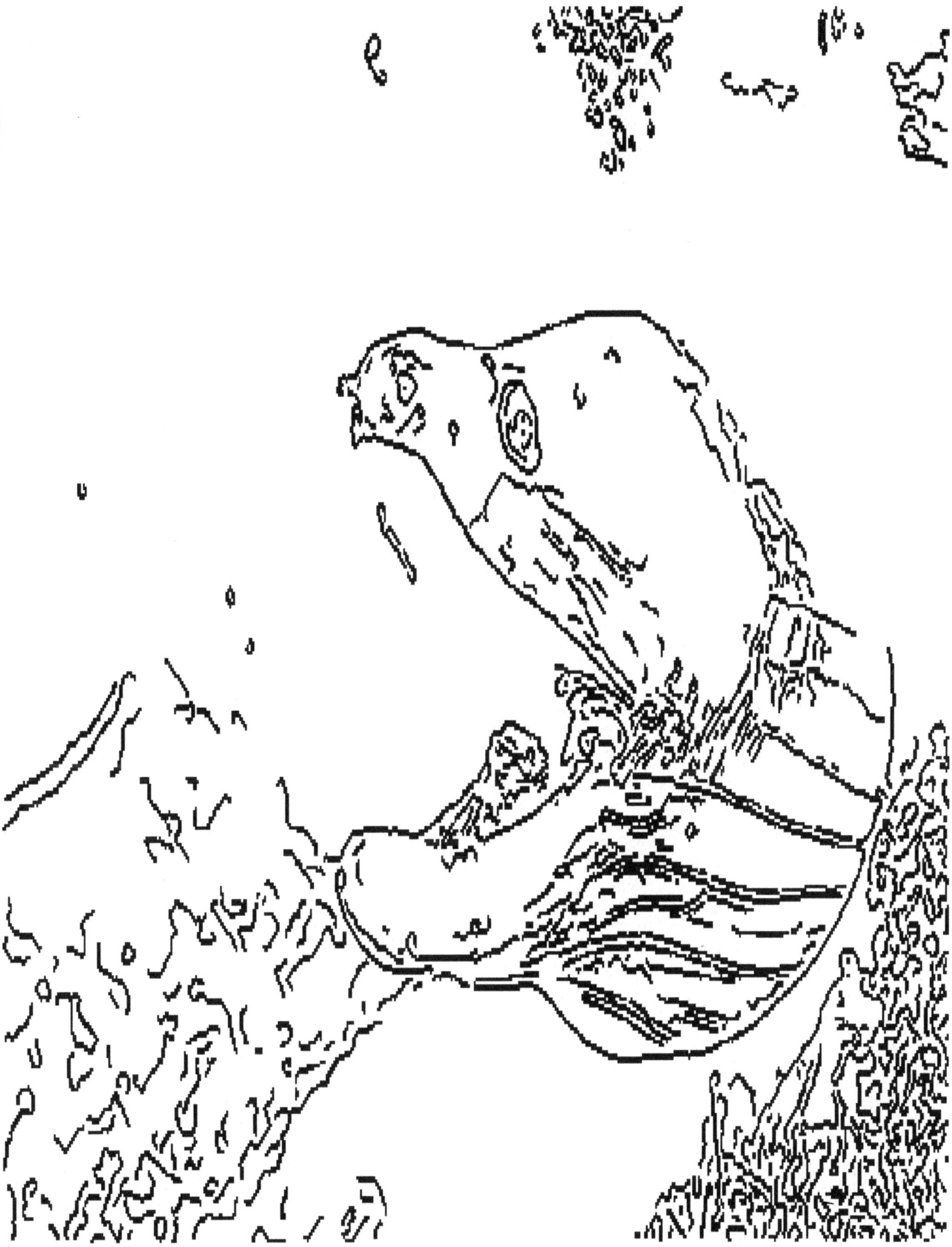

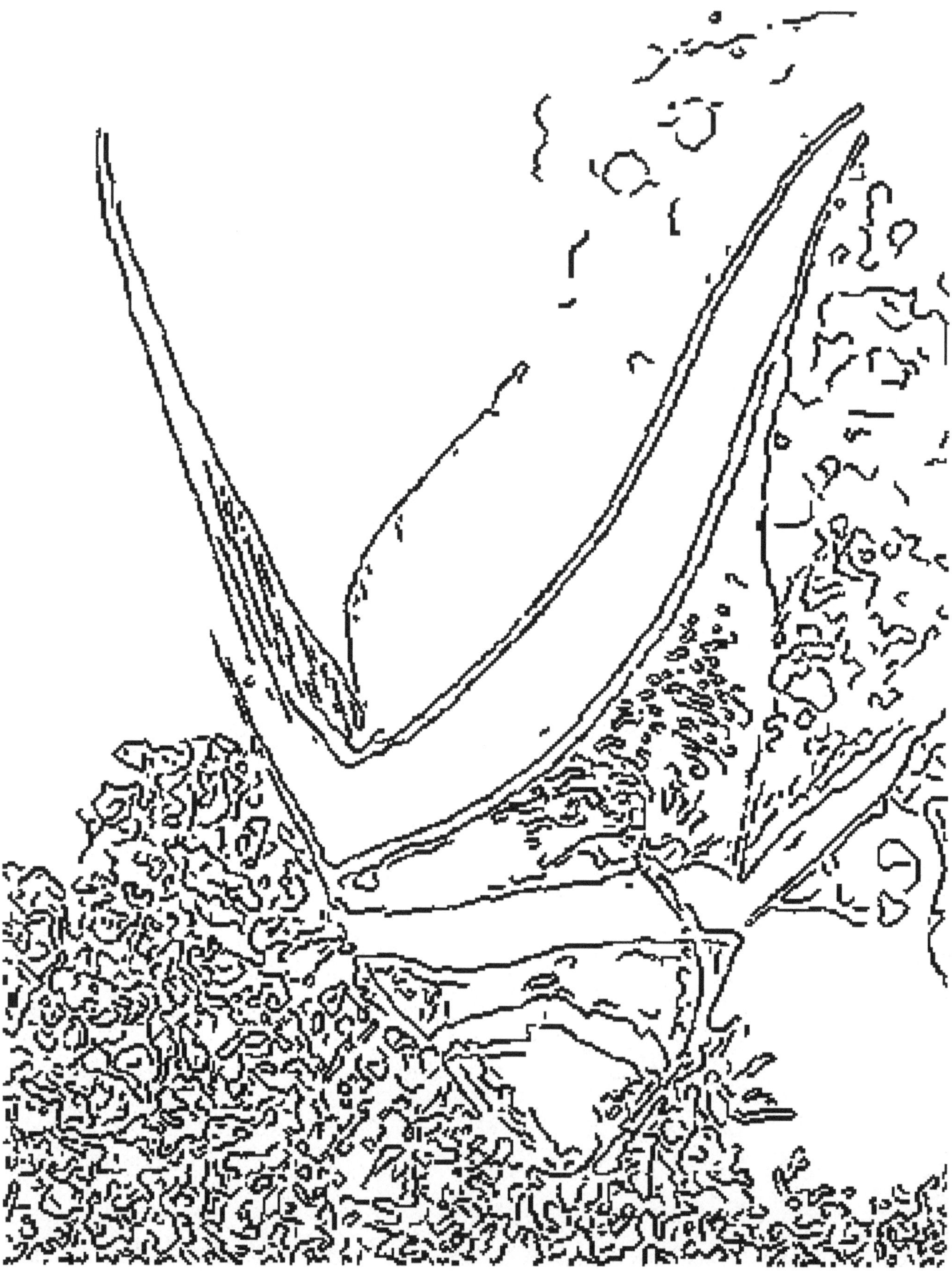

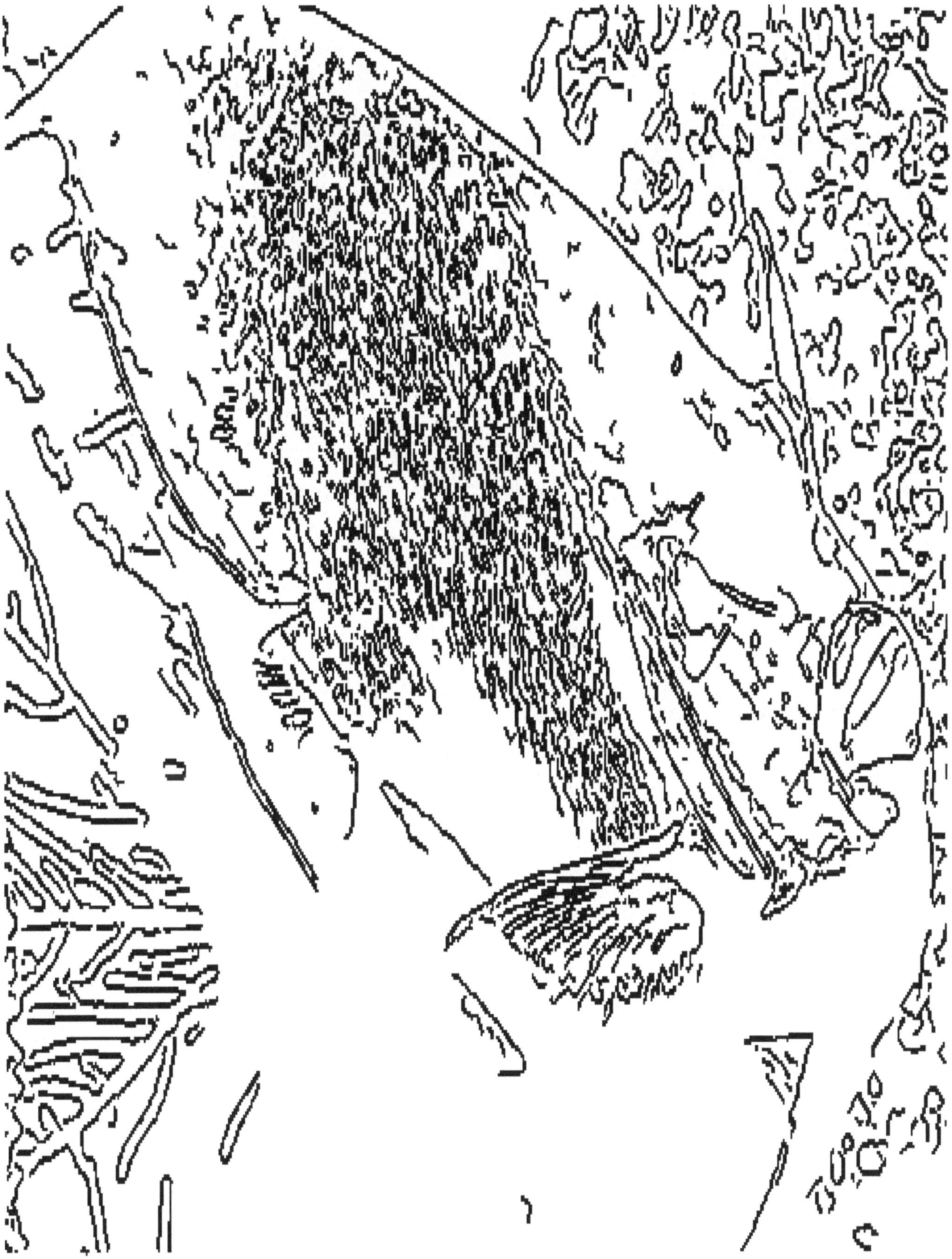

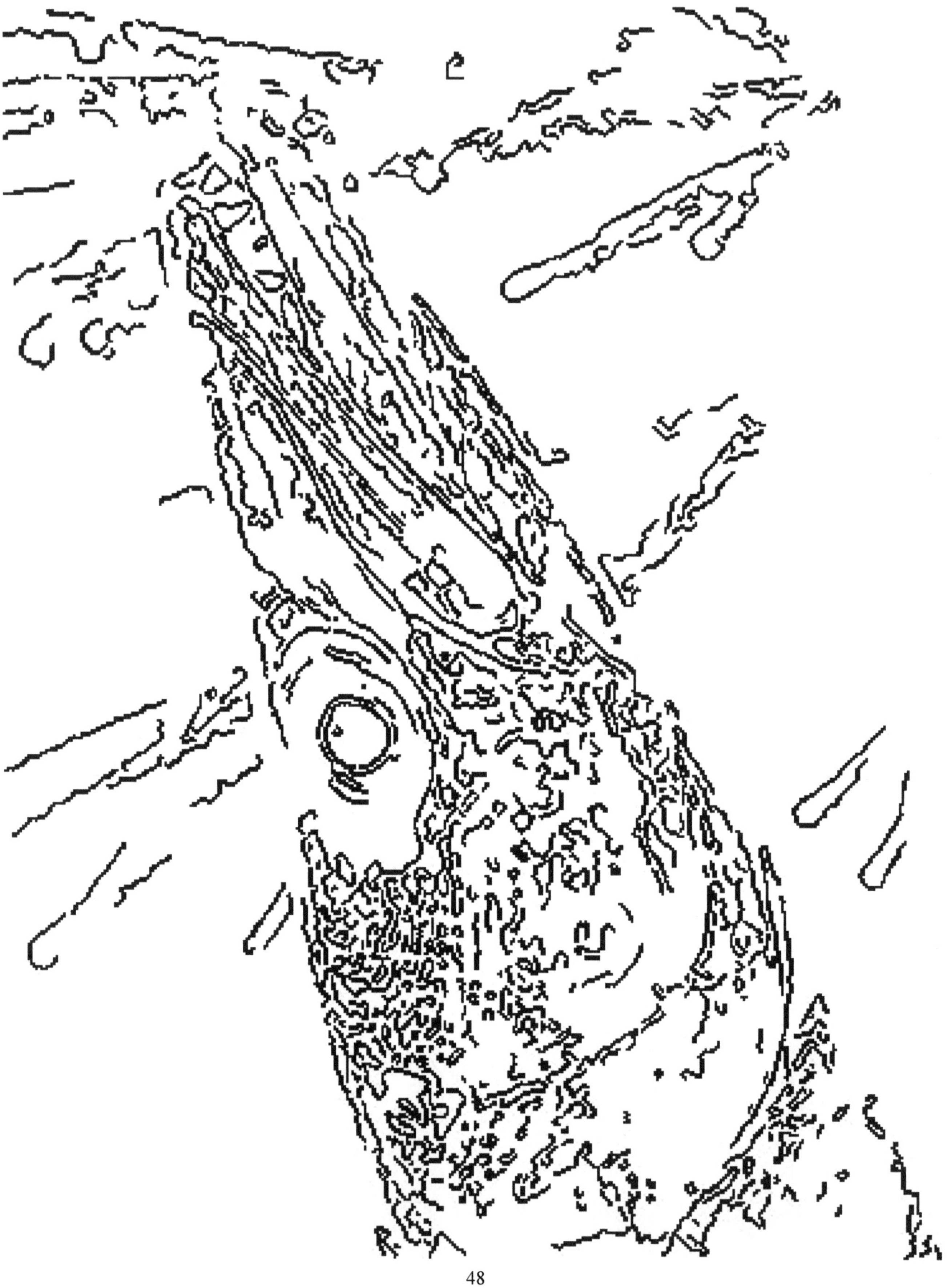

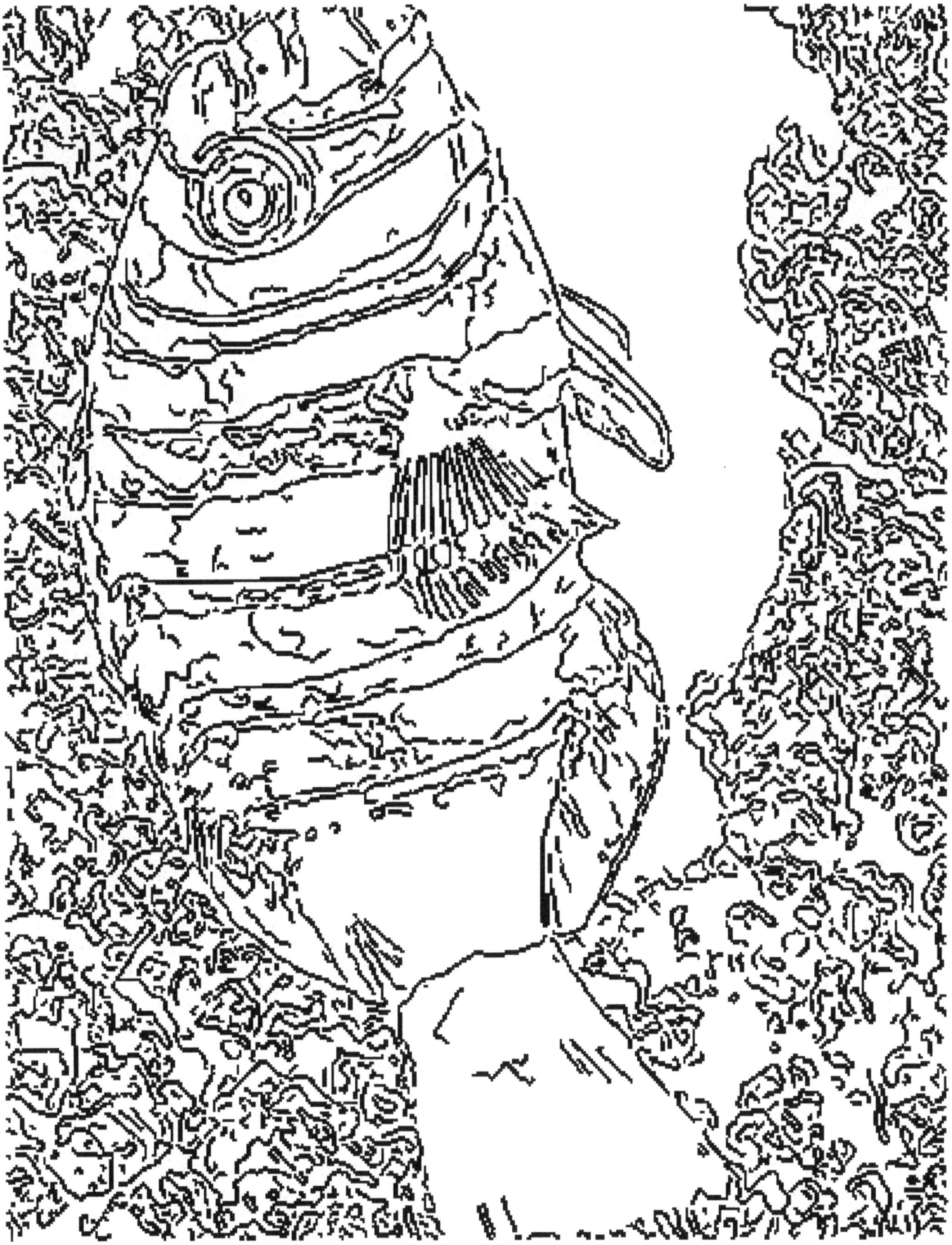

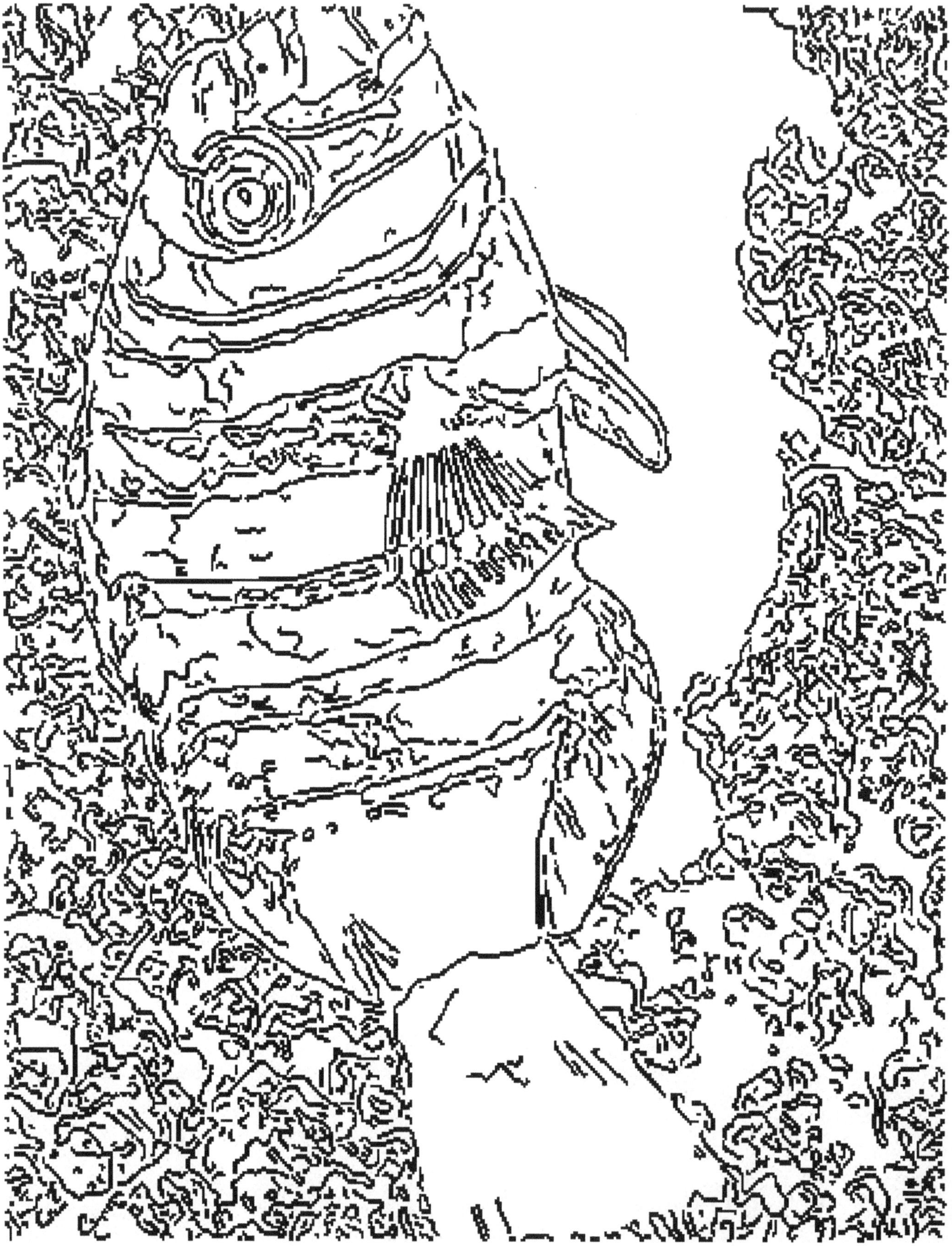

www.ingramcontent.com/pod-product-compliance
Lightning Source LLC
Chambersburg PA
CBHW040745200526
45159CB00023B/1729

* 9 7 8 1 5 2 3 7 1 5 1 6 9 *